A GARDEN OF PRAYERS

This book (in its entirety) is dedicated to Jesus Christ, Son of the Living God. It is His book. I am simply the vessel He chose to write it, (Halleluiah!) and I am so very grateful for Him using me! Praise His holy, precious, and mighty Name forevermore!

These prayers were birthed out of an intense time of warfare, of which Jesus won the victory, of course! Amen! So I have lived these prayers, cried out to God in pure desperation through these prayers, and always seen Him remain faithful to the end! Praise God! I can promise you that our God cannot fail you, regardless of what your circumstances appear to be right now! No mountain is too big for Him to handle! He is the Great I Am, the Beginning and the End, and the Alpha and the Omega! Glory to the King of kings and the Lord of lords!

I encourage you to read, pray, and claim these prayers over you and your entire families, and just watch how God moves on your behalf! Remember to never tell God how big your problem is. Instead, always tell your problem how BIG your God is! Amen!

Blessings! I am praying for you!

CONTENTS

1.

Dear God, I HUMBLY repent for my family, my spouse's and my ancestors (on both sides of the family), ALL of our future generations, myself, and everybody and everything under my spouse's and my covering – for ALL of our sins (past, present, and future, PERMANENTLY and FOREVER) – intentional or unintentional. We ask You to wash us spotlessly clean through Your saving grace and holy righteousness. I humbly ask You to redeem All of our sins with endtime anointings in unlimited measure, such as this world has never seen before! I soak this prayer in the BLOOD of Jesus, the HOLY anointing oil of the Holy Ghost, and the FIRE of God, in Jesus' Name. Amen.

2.

Dear God, I ask YOU to break off ALL word curses (PAST, PRESENT, and FUTURE, PERMANENTLY and FOREVER!) spoken over (or by) my family, my spouse's and my ancestors (on both sides of the family), myself, and everybody and everything under my spouse's and my covering. I ask YOU – in the precious, mighty, matchless Name of Jesus – to redeem ALL of these word curses with endtime anointings in unlimited measure, such as this world has never seen before – for Your Name's sake. I soak this prayer in the blood of Jesus, the holy anointing oil of the Holy Ghost, and the fire of God, in Jesus' Name. Amen.

3.

Dear God, I ask You to cover my family, my spouse's and my ancestors (on BOTH sides of the family), ALL of our future generations, myself, and everybody and everything under my spouse's and my covering – spirit, soul, and body, including ALL prayers prayed BY us (or FOR us); ALL electronic devices – such as computers, phones, and TVs; vehicles – including the body as well as ALL of the mechanics; security of ANY kind whatsoever; godly relationships – ordained by God Himself; our moods, temperaments, emotions, giftings, callings, destinies, and prophecies; and ALL personal information – in the Name of the FATHER, the SON, and the HOLY GHOST.

I ask You – in the Name of Your precious, HOLY Son – to redeem ALL attacks against us (past, present, and future, permanently and forever) with endtime anointings in unlimited measure, such as this world has never seen before! I soak this prayer in the BLOOD of Jesus, the HOLY anointing oil of the Holy Ghost, and the FIRE of God, in Jesus' Name. Amen.

4.

Dear God, I lift up to You – in the Mighty, Mighty, Mighty Name of our precious Lord and Savior, Jesus Christ – ALL relationships of my family, my spouse's and my ancestors (on both sides of the family), myself, and everybody and everything under my spouse's and my covering – past, present, and future. I ask You to break ALL ties to anybody or anything that are not from You, and I ask You to bind us to Your heart and to ALL the things of Your heart! I pray this prayer in the Mighty, Mighty, Mighty Name of our precious Lord and Savior, Jesus Christ.

We ask You to redeem (with endtime anointings in unlimited measure, such as this world has never seen before!) ALL of our ungodly relationships – for Your Name's sake, to strengthen (with supernatural Holy Ghost power) ALL of our godly relationships – in the Name of our precious Lord and Savior, Jesus Christ, and to build new, lasting relationships that are pre-ordained in heaven – that bring honor and glory to God Most High and put a smile on His face. I soak this prayer in the blood of Jesus, the holy anointing oil of the Holy Ghost, and the fire of God, in Jesus' Name. Amen.

5.

Dear God, I lift up to You – in the Mighty, Mighty, Mighty
Name of Jesus, that Name which is above ALL names (to
which ALL knees shall bow in heaven, on earth, and
under the earth) – all doors in the lives of my family, my
spouse's and my ancestors (on both sides of the family),
myself, and everybody and everything under my
spouse's and my covering. We pray that You open All
the doors that YOU want opened and You shut ALL the
doors that YOU want shut, in Jesus' Name! We thank
You, in advance, for answering this prayer, and we give
You ALL the glory, praise, and honor for this, in the
precious, mighty, matchless Name of Jesus, King of kings
and Lord of lords!

We humbly repent for our involvement in ANY of these
doors being wrongfully opened or shut, and we ask for
full forgiveness, in Jesus' Name. I humbly ask You to
redeem ALL the wrong doors that have either been
opened or shut that were not supposed to be, with
endtime anointings in unlimited measure, such as this
world has never seen before! I soak this prayer in the
blood of Jesus, the holy anointing oil of the Holy Ghost,
and the fire of God, in Jesus' Name. Amen.

6.

Dear God, I lift up to You – in the precious, holy, and Mighty Name of Jesus – ALL breakthroughs in the lives of my family, my spouse's and my ancestors (on both sides of the family), myself, and everybody and everything under my spouse's and my covering (past, present, and future). I humbly ask You to "make a way where there is no way", to permanently remove ALL blockages that have been preventing us from moving into our Promised Land, and to literally EXPLODE us into our pre-ordained destinies INSTANTLY!!! I PRAISE You for Your goodness and faithfulness, for safely carrying us this far and know that You will surely continue to do so for Your Name's sake!

We humbly ask You – in the MIGHTY, MIGHTY, MIGHTY Name of Jesus – to redeem ALL things that have kept us back from fulfilling YOUR destiny in US, with endtime anointings in unlimited measure, such as this world has never seen before! I soak this prayer in the blood of Jesus, the holy anointing oil of the Holy Ghost, and the fire of God, in Jesus' Name. Amen.

7.

Dear God, I would like to lift up to You – in the precious, matchless, Mighty Name of Jesus Christ, who reigns forevermore – ALL blessings in the lives of my family, my spouse's and my ancestors (on both sides of the family), myself, and everybody and everything under my spouse's and my covering. I humbly ask You to pour out upon us – in unlimited measure – ALL the blessings that YOU have stored up for us, "for such a time as this". We fully acknowledge that ALL of these blessings come from YOU alone, and YOU freely give them to whomever (and however) YOU choose! We fall on our faces before You in humble adoration for Who You are! We worship and adore YOU as the Lord of our lives and humbly come before YOU with overflowing, grateful hearts! We thank YOU and praise YOU for Your abundant goodness and favor! May we always give glory "where glory is due" and NEVER even TRY to share YOUR glory with another, ESPECIALLY with ourselves!!! We humbly ask YOU to redeem ALL things that have held back YOUR blessings from being poured out upon us, with endtime anointings in unlimited measure, such as this world has never seen before! I soak this prayer in the blood of Jesus, the holy anointing oil of the Holy Ghost, and the fire of God, in Jesus' Name. Amen.

8.

Dear God, I HUMBLY repent for my family, my spouse's and my ancestors (on both sides of the family), ALL of our future generations, myself, and everybody and everything under my spouse's and my covering – for 7 HIGHLY offensive sins, namely: jealousy, unforgiveness, condemnation, rebellion, deception, low self-esteem, and pride (past, present, and future, permanently and forever). I ask You to wash us SPOTLESSLY clean through Your saving grace and holy righteousness. We receive (by faith) Your FULL forgiveness of these sins in our lives, and we ask that You give us "clean hands and pure hearts". We pray that You redeem these grevious sins – for Your HOLY, precious Name's sake – with endtime anointings in unlimited measure, such as this world has never seen before! I soak this prayer in the BLOOD of Jesus, the HOLY anointing oil of the Holy Ghost, and the FIRE of God, in Jesus' Name. Amen.

9.

Dear God, my family, my spouse's and my ancestors (on both sides of the family), all of our future generations, I, and everybody and everything under my spouse's and my covering lift up holy hands to You. We give You our EVERYTHING and declare that YOU ALONE are our everything! We praise and worship YOU, for You ALONE are the One TRUE God! We join with all of Your angelic hosts and the saints in Glory to honor and exalt KING JESUS! There is NONE like You in heaven, on the earth, or under the earth! You ARE the Greatest Treasure of all! You are the Alpha and the Omega, the Beginning and the End! NOTHING exists outside of You! You are our very sustenance! Each breath even comes from You! We break the sound barrier in shouting our praises to You – the King of kings and the Lord of lords – for You ALONE are worthy!

We HUMBLY LAY DOWN our lives for YOU, on YOUR holy altar. Use us wholly for YOUR purposes and glory – to make YOUR Name famous throughout the ends of the earth! Redeem EVERYTHING in us that has not been used for YOU, with endtime anointings in unlimited measure, such as this world has never seen before! I soak this prayer in the blood of Jesus, the holy anointing oil of the Holy Ghost, and the fire of God, in Jesus' Name. Amen.

10.

Dear God, we – my family, my spouse's and my ancestors (on BOTH sides of the family), all of our future generations, I, and everybody and everything under my spouse's and my covering – humbly come to You with a VERY special request today. We would like to ask You for the gift of faith, for we know that faith pleases You, and the GREATEST desire of our hearts is to please YOU! Now, we are not asking for just a little bit of faith, for we want to please You beyond COMPREHENSION! We know that You are a GIANT-SIZED God, and so we are asking for a GIANT-SIZED dose of YOUR faith! Attend Your ears to our cries, we pray! – in the MIGHTY, MATCHLESS Name of Jesus!

Redeem ALL of our lack of faith for Your glory, I pray, with endtime anointings in unlimited measure, such as this world has NEVER seen before! I soak this prayer in the blood of Jesus, the holy anointing oil of the Holy Ghost, and the fire of God, in Jesus' Name. Amen.

11.

Dear Mighty God, I would like to lift up to You – in the
Precious, Holy, and Sovereign Name of Jesus – my
family, my spouse's and my ancestors (on BOTH sides of
the family), ALL of our future generations, myself, and
everybody and everything under my spouse's and my
covering. We would like to HUMBLY ask You for one
more thing today. Jesus, we know that in the Lord's
Prayer, You tell us to "forgive our debtors". Jesus, You
exemplified this on the cross when You asked Your
Father to forgive Your murderers. So we want to forgive
as You forgave. Please give us the gift of forgiveness, we
pray – in the Mighty, Majestic, and Sovereign Name of
our Lord and Savior, Jesus Christ!

Please redeem ALL of our unforgiveness – for YOUR
Name's sake – with endtime anointings in unlimited
measure, such as this world has NEVER see before! I
soak this prayer in the blood of Jesus, the holy anointing
oil of the Holy Ghost, and the fire of God, in Jesus' Name.
Amen.

12.

Dear God, we – my family, my spouse's and my ancestors (on BOTH sides of the family), ALL of our future generations, I, and everybody and everything under my spouse's and my covering – HUMBLY come to You with one last request today. We would like to ask You for the VERY special gift of purity – straight from YOUR heart to ours, like PURE, liquid gold being poured into us until we overflow JESUS!!! When others look at us, may they see ONLY YOU!!! YOU ARE our ALL in ALL! Our PUREST desire is to be EXACT mirror reflections of YOU! We want YOU to be glorified in ALL that we think, do, or say!

Please redeem EVERYTHING in us that does not look smell, sound, or feel like You – for Your HOLY Name's sake – with endtime anointings in unlimited measure, such as this world has never seen before! I soak this prayer in the blood of Jesus, the holy anointing oil of the Holy Ghost, and the fire of God, in Jesus' Name. Amen.

Request for Greater Holy Ghost Giftings

Dear God, we – my family, my spouse's and my ancestors (on BOTH sides of the family), ALL of our future generations, I, and everybody and everything under my spouse's and my covering – would like to ask You for something very special now. You know that we are living in the end times and so require greater giftings, which come from YOU ALONE! Our 7 requests are as follows: UNLIMITED Holy Ghost power from on high, PURE Christ-likeness, the TRUE Father heart of God, Your COMPLETE and PERFECT sanity, the mind of Christ, supernatural guards over our mouths at all times, and to work, in all things, "as unto the Lord". Redeem – for Your holy Name's sake – anything and everything (past, present, and future, PERMANENTLY and FOREVER!) that has come against these very specific requests, with endtime anointings in unlimited measure, such as this world has NEVER seen before! I soak this prayer in the BLOOD of Jesus, the HOLY anointing oil of the Holy Ghost, and the FIRE of God, in Jesus' Name. Amen.

King Jesus' Incense

Dear God, I would like to lift up to You – in the Precious, Holy, and MIGHTY NAME of JESUS, that NAME which is above ALL names (to whom ALL knees shall bow, in HEAVEN, on the EARTH, and UNDER THE EARTH!) – all time, jobs, and ministry. We know that these ALL belong to YOU! They are held SECURELY in YOUR righteous, right hand, and You do with them as YOU please – bringing HONOR and GLORY to YOUR Holy, Precious, MIGHTY Name! Please provide these 3 things in ABUNDANCE to YOUR people, for YOUR Name's sake, we pray this.

Redeem EVERYTHING that has come against ANY and ALL of these things – for YOUR Name's sake, we pray this – with endtime anointings in UNLIMITED measure, such as this world has NEVER seen before! We SOAK this prayer in the precious, holy, and MIGHTY NAME of JESUS; the precious, holy, and MIGHTY NAME of the HOLY GHOST; and the precious, holy, and MIGHTY NAME of GOD the FATHER MOST HIGH! AMEN!

Request for Finances and Strength

Dear PRECIOUS, HOLY, and MIGHTY, SOVEREIGN GOD
of the UNIVERSE, we HUMBLY come before You with our
faces to the ground, acknowledging YOU as Sovereign
LORD and CREATOR of our lives! We declare that YOU
ALONE are worthy of ALL of our PRAISE and
ADORATION! There is NONE like You in ALL of the
earth! We CRY out with the angels, DAY and NIGHT,
saying, "HOLY, HOLY, HOLY are YOU, KING JESUS (who
sits on the throne), to receive POWER and RICHES and
WISDOM and STRENGTH and HONOR and GLORY and
BLESSINGS FOREVER and EVER! AMEN!"

We acknowledge that ALL GOOD THINGS come from
YOU, and YOU ALONE, and we PRAISE, HONOR, and
EXALT Your PRECIOUS, HOLY, and MIGHTY Name for
that! PLEASE bless YOUR people with finances and
strength – in SUPER ABUNDANCE – (for YOUR Name's
sake) IN ORDER to further YOUR KINGDOM here "on
earth as it is in heaven"! Only YOU have the UNLIMITED
RESOURCES needed to accomplish YOUR purposes, here
on earth, during these end times! May we be FAITHFUL
STEWARDS of ALL that You entrust to us – in the
MIGHTY, HOLY, and PRECIOUS Name of Jesus! – and

use it FULLY to bring honor, praise, and glory to Your MATCHLESS, PRECIOUS, and HOLY Name, KING JESUS! We HUMBLY ask YOU to redeem EVERYTHING that has come against YOUR finances and YOUR strength – in YOUR people – with ENDTIME anointings in UNLIMITED measure, such as this world has NEVER seen before! We SOAK this prayer in the BLOOD of JESUS, the HOLY anointing oil of the HOLY GHOST, and the FIRE of GOD, in JESUS' NAME. AMEN.

Request for Wisdom

Dear Holy, Precious, MIGHTY, and SOVEREIGN MAKER of ALL, we HUMBLY come before Your presence with THANKSGIVING and enter YOUR courts with PRAISE! To YOU ALONE belongs all HONOR, GLORY, DOMINION, and POWER! There is NONE like You in ALL the earth! WORTHY, WORTHY, WORTHY are You, KING JESUS! We BOW our knees TO YOU and WORSHIP in YOUR sweet, holy Presence! Our PUREST DELIGHT is to COMMUNE with YOU! HOLY, HOLY, HOLY is the LORD GOD ALMIGHTY! The WHOLE EARTH is FILLED with YOUR GLORY! HALLELUIAH!

Dear Jesus, we HUMBLY lay our requests at YOUR feet, for YOU ALONE are ABLE (and WILLING) to grant our requests. It is YOUR DELIGHT when Your children rely upon YOU for their needs (and wants) to be met, for YOU ALONE can PROVIDE!

Today, our desires are: for our eyes to be OPENED to YOUR TRUTHS, for YOUR WISDOM, KNOWLEDGE, and UNDERSTANDING to be poured out upon us in UNLIMITED MEASURE, and for our hearts to be FULLY

and COMPLETELY RECEPTIVE to YOU and to ALL that
YOU have for us – in the precious, MIGHTY, and
MATCHLESS NAME of JESUS! We VERY HUMBLY ask
YOU to redeem ANYTHING and EVERYTHING that has
blocked these requests from FULLY manifesting – in the
very, VERY MIGHTY NAME of our Lord and Savior, JESUS
CHRIST! – with endtime anointings in unlimited measure,
such as this world has NEVER seen before! We SOAK
this prayer in the BLOOD of JESUS, the HOLY anointing
oil of the HOLY GHOST, and the FIRE of GOD, in JESUS'
NAME. AMEN.

Requests for the Endtime Harvest

Dear PERCIOUS, HOLY, and MIGHTY, SOVEREIGN GOD
of the UNIVERSE, we HUMBLY come before YOU with
GRATEFUL hearts, acknowledging YOU as KING of our
LIVES (past, present, and future, PERMANENTLY and
FOREVER!) as YOU REIGN SUPERME over ALL! We
BOW DOWN, at Your feet, to WORSHIP and ADORE the
LORD of HOSTS! We EXALT YOUR HOLY, PRECIOUS
NAME ABOVE the heavens, for YOU ALONE are
WORTHY to be PRAISED FOREVERMORE! AMEN!

Our HUMBLE requests are as follows: WILLING workers,
a MASSIVE harvest (such as this world has NEVER seen
before!), PERFECT, UNDIVIDED, and CHRIST-LIKE UNITY
in the Body of Christ, and COMPLETE, UNASHAMED, and
RADICAL LAID-DOWN LOVERS of JESUS CHRIST
ALMIGHTY!

We HUMBLY ask YOU to redeem ALL evil that has come
against these VERY specific requests – in the PRECIOUS,
MIGHTY, and MATCHLESS NAME of JESUS! – with
ENDTIME ANOINTINGS in UNLIMITED MEASURE, such as
this world has NEVER SEEN BEFORE! We SOAK this

prayer in the BLOOD of JESUS, the HOLY ANOINTING OIL of the HOLY GHOST, and the FIRE of GOD, in JESUS' NAME. AMEN.

Request for Cleanliness

Dear PRECIOUS, HOLY, and MIGHTY, SOVEREIGN GOD of the UNIVERSE, You are WORHTY to be PRAISED ABOVE ALL peoples, nations, and tongues! We EXALT Your HOLY, PRECIOUS, and MATCHLESS NAME above the HIGHEST HEAVEN, for YOU ALONE are WORTHY to be PRAISED! There is NONE like YOU in heaven, on the earth, or under the earth! YOU ALONE STAND clothed in RADIANT SPLENDOR and MAJESTY! The WHOLE EARTH is FILLED with YOUR GLORY! ALL PRAISE, HONOR, and MAJESTY BELONG to YOU, KING JESUS! We STAND to our FEET and APPLAUD the EVERLASTING LORD and SAVIOR of our LIVES, Who LIVES FOREVERMORE! AMEN!

Our requests today are SIMPLE: for us to be THOROUGHLY and COMPLETELY washed CLEAN by the BLOOD of JESUS, for us to be REDEEMED by the BLOOD of the LAMB, and for us to have YOUR TRUTHS and REVELATIONS EXPLODE DEEP into our VERY BEINGS (past, present, and future, PERMANENTLY and FOREVER!)! We pray this in the PRECIOUS, MIGHTY, and SOVEREIGN Name of our LORD and SAVIOR, JESUS CHRIST! We HUMBLY ask You to REDEEM ANYTHING and EVERYTHING that has come against these VERY SPECIFIC REQUESTS – in the PRECIOUS, MIGHTY, and MATCHLESS NAME of JESUS – with ENDTIME ANOINTINGS in UNLIMITED MEASURE, such as this world has NEVER SEEN BEFORE! We SOAK this PRAYER in the BLOOD of JESUS, the HOLY ANOINTING OIL of the HOLY GHOST, and the FIRE of GOD, in JESUS' NAME! AMEN!

Request for Mighty, Godly Leaders

Dear God ALMIGHTY, LORD of HEAVEN and EARTH, we PRAISE Your HOLY, MIGHTY, and PRECIOUS NAME – for YOU ALONE are WORTHY to be PRAISED ABOVE ALL PEOPLES, NATIONS, and TONGUES! To YOU ALONE do we ascribe BEAUTY, HONOR, MAJESTY, AUTHORTIY, POWER, DOMINION, and PRAISE! There is NONE like YOU in heaven, on the earth, or under the earth! The WHOLE EARTH is FILLED with YOUR GLORY! All PRAISE, HONOR, and ADORATION belong to YOU ALONE! YOU are WORTHY, KING JESUS!

We HUMBLY, HUMBLY come to You, today, with only ONE request: for YOU to raise up MIGHTY, GODLY leaders to help lead YOUR people during these end times! May they have ONE FOCUS, and ONE FOCUS ONLY – and that is JESUS, JESUS, JESUS! May their DESIRE be for YOU ALONE! – to HONOR, SERVE, and PLEASE YOU ALL THE DAYS OF THEIR LIVES, here on earth, with EVERY LAST DROP of THEIR BEING! Let their EVERY THOUGHT, WORD, and DEED be OF, FOR, and BY YOU, KING JESUS! May they be TOTALLY and COMPLETELY FEARLESS for YOU, KING JESUS! – FEARLESS of what man MAY or MAY NOT THINK, DO, or

SAY, FEARLESS of the DEMONIC, and FEARLESS of ANYTHING AT ALL – except for a RIGHT, HOLY FEAR of GOD HIMSELF! We HUMBLY ask You, dear JESUS (LORD of our LIVES and of ALL THAT EXISTS), to redeem ALL things that have come against YOU, and YOU ALONE, in regards to this request – with ENDTIME ANOINTINGS in UNLIMITED MEASURE, such as this world has NEVER SEEN BEFORE! We SOAK this prayer in the BLOOD of JESUS, the HOLY anointing oil of the HOLY GHOST, and the FIRE of GOD, in JESUS' NAME. AMEN.

OUR GOD IS NOT MOVED!

DEAR HOLY, PRECIOUS, AND MIGHTY GOD OF ALL
CREATION, YOU ALONE ARE WORTHY TO BE
HONORED, PRAISED, AND ADORED FOREVERMORE!
AMEN! TO YOU ALONE DO WE GIVE OUR
EVERYTHING, FOR YOU ARE WORTHY OF IT ALL!
PRAISE YOU, PRAISE YOU, PRAISE YOU IN THE
HIGHEST! LET EVERYTHING THAT HAS BREATH, PRAISE
THE LORD! PRAISE HIM IN THE MORNING, PRAISE HIM
IN THE AFTERNOON, AND PRAISE HIM IN THE
EVENING! HALLELUIAH!

GOD, WE WOULD LIKE TO LIFT UP TO YOU THE
SUBJECT MATTER OF BEING POSITIVE! WE KNOW
THAT YOU ARE ALWAYS POSITIVE REGARDING EACH
AND EVERY SITUATION BECAUSE YOU SEE IT FROM UP
ABOVE! YOU ARE SEATED IN HEAVENLY PLACES AND
KNOW (WITHOUT A SHADOW OF A DOUBT) THAT –
LITERALLY – ALL THINGS ARE POSSIBLE THROUGH YOU,
KING JESUS! YOU ARE NEVER WORRIED, FEARFUL, OR
IN DOUBT! YOU ARE NOT MOVED BY
CIRCUMSTANCES! YOU STAY FOREVER (PAST, PRSENT,
AND FUTURE, PERMANENTLY AND FOREVER!) THE
SAME! HALLELUIAH! SO WE DESIRE TO SEE THINGS AS

YOU SEE THEM, TO PUT OUR COMPLETE AND
ABSOLUTE TRUST IN YOU – AND YOU ALONE, AND TO
WALK (AND LIVE) IN YOUR PERFECT PEACE – THAT
PASSES ALL UNDERSTANDING – ALL THE DAYS OF OUR
LIVES FOREVER AND EVER! AMEN! WE ASK YOU NOW,
DEAR JESUS, TO REDEEM EVERYTHING NEGATIVE IN
OUR LIVES! (PAST, PRESENT, AND FUTURE,
PERMANENTLY AND FOREVER!) WITH ENDTIME
ANOINTINGS IN UNLIMITED MEASURE, SUCH AS THIS
WORLD HAS NEVER SEEN BEFORE! WE SOAK THIS
PRAYER IN THE BLOOD OF JESUS, THE HOLY
ANOINTING OIL OF THE HOLY GHOST, AND THE FIRE
OF GOD, IN JESUS' NAME! AMEN!

OUR GOD IS COMPLETELY WHOLE!

DEAR HOLY, PRECIOUS, AND MIGHTY SOVEREIGN GOD OF THE UNIVERSE, YOU ARE AWESOME IN THIS PLACE, MIGHTY GOD! HOW WE PRAISE AND LIFT YOU HIGH, HOLY GOD! YOU ALONE ARE KING SUPREME! THERE IS NONE LIKE JEHOVAH! HOW WE WORSHIP AT YOUR FEET, PRECIOUS LORD! YOU ALONE ARE GOD! YOU ALONE ARE GOD! YOU ALONE ARE GOD, WHOM WE ADORE!

OUR NEXT REQUEST – TO YOU – TODAY, IS THE MATTER OF WHOLENESS! (SPIRIT, SOUL, AND BODY!)! WE ASK YOU, DEAR AND PRECIOUS SAVIOR, TO COME INVADE OUR LIVES FULLY AND COMPLETELY WITH YOUR PRESENCE! (PAST, PRESENT, AND FUTURE, PERMANENTLY AND FOREVER!)! LET US BE SO FULL OF YOU, JESUS, THAT NO SICKNESS, DISEASE, OR INJURY CAN EVEN COME CLOSE TO US OR ANYBODY OR ANYTHING THAT YOU HAVE ENTRUSTED TO OUR CARE! MAY WE LIVE, MOVE, AND HAVE OUR BEING IN CHRIST JESUS, OUR LORD! MAY WE BE IN SUCH CLOSE COMMUNION WITH YOU – AT ALL TIMES – THAT WE STAY UNDER YOUR HEDGE OF PROTECTION (LIKE A HOLY GHOST BUBBLE!)! REDEEM, WE PRAY, ANYTHING

AND EVERYTHING THAT HAS COME AGAINST YOUR WHOLENESS, IN US, WITH ENDTIME ANOINTINGS IN UNLIMITED MEASURE, SUCH AS THIS WORLD HAS NEVER SEEN BEFORE! WE SOAK THIS PRAYER IN THE BLOOD OF JESUS, THE HOLY ANOINTING OIL OF THE HOLY GHOST, AND THE FIRE OF GOD, IN JESUS' NAME! AMEN!

OUR GOD HAS UNLIMITED RESOURCES!

DEAR GOD ALMIGHTY, WHO IS FULL OF POWER AND GLORY, WE GIVE YOU ALL PRAISE, HONOR, AND WORSHIP – FOR YOU ALONE ARE WORTHY OF OUR EVERYTHING! WE LAY OUR LIVES BEFORE YOU – ON YOUR HOLY ALTAR – TO MAGNIFY YOUR HOLY AND PRECIOUS NAME! RECEIVE OUR PRAISE NOW, OH LORD, WE PRAY!

OUR LAST REQUEST FOR THE DAY IS PURE AND SIMPLE ABUNDANCE, IN UNLIMITED MEASURE, SUCH AS THIS WORLD HAS NEVER SEEN BEFORE! YOU ARE THE GOD OF UNLIMITED RESOURCES, SO NOTHING IS TOO HARD FOR YOU! WE HUMBLY ASK YOU, LORD OF EVERYTHING, TO POUR OUT YOUR RESOURCES INTO YOUR KINGDOM, HERE, "ON EARTH, AS IT IS IN HEAVEN", FOR "THINE IS THE KINGDOM AND THE POWER AND THE GLORY FOREVER! AMEN!"

REDEEM, WE PRAY, ALL LACK – FOR YOUR HOLY AND PRECIOUS NAME'S SAKE – WITH ENDTIME ANOINTINGS IN UNLIMITED MEASURE, SUCH AS THIS WORLD HAS NEVER SEEN BEFORE! WE SOAK THIS PRAYER IN THE

BLOOD OF JESUS, THE HOLY ANOINTING OIL OF THE HOLY GHOST, AND THE FIRE OF GOD, IN JESUS' NAME! AMEN!

James 1:2-8

2. Consider it pure joy, my brothers, whenever you face trials of many kinds, 3. because you know that the testing of your faith develops perseverance. 4. Perseverance must finish its work so that you may be mature and complete, not lacking anything. 5. If any of you lacks wisdom, he should ask God, who gives generously to all without finding fault, and it will be given to him. 6. But when he asks, he must believe and not doubt, because he who doubts is like a wave of the sea, blown and tossed by the wind. 7. That man should not think he will receive anything from the Lord; 8. He is a double-minded man, unstable in all he does.

Dear Heavenly Father, Lord of ALL creation, we worship and adore YOUR holy Name – for You ALONE are worthy of ALL praise, honor, and adoration! There is NONE like You in heaven, on the earth, or under the earth! ALL of creation gives YOU glory and praise! We join with YOUR angels in heaven in singing YOUR praises! "HOSANNAH in the Highest! HOSANNAH in the Highest! GLORY to the King of kings!"

Our desire is to LOOK like You, Precious Savior – in ALL aspects. May the world see JESUS, and Jesus ONLY, when they look at us! May we be SO like You, that people are naturally drawn to YOU and give YOU all the glory, honor, and praise! We thank YOU for molding us into YOUR perfect image, so that we may be perfect and complete, lacking NOTHING! Lord Jesus, please give us YOUR patience, perfection, and wisdom, we pray now – in the MATCHLESS, PRECIOUS, and HOLY Name of Jesus! Redeem ANYTHING and EVERYTHING that has come against these requests – in the HOLY, PRECIOUS, and MIGHTY NAME OF JESUS – with endtime ANOINTINGS in UNLIMITED measure, such as this world has NEVER seen before! We SOAK this prayer in the blood of JESUS, the holy anointing oil of the HOLY GHOST, and the fire of GOD, in JESUS' NAME! AMEN!

Jude 20-21

20. But you, dear friends, build yourselves up in your most holy faith and pray in the Holy Spirit. 21. Keep yourselves in God's love as you wait for the mercy of our Lord Jesus Christ to bring you to eternal life.

Dear Heavenly Father, Sovereign and Mighty Lord of ALL that exists, we worship at YOUR holy throne, proclaiming YOU as King Supreme! There is NONE like our Precious JESUS in ALL of the entire universe! GLORY to the LORD of HOSTS! GLORY to the KING of KINGS! WORTHY, WORTHY, WORTHY, are YOU, Lord God Almighty! We exalt YOUR holy, precious Name in ALL the earth, declaring YOU as Lord of all!

Our BURNING desire is to be in YOUR holy presence, worshipping at YOUR holy feet. We ask YOU now, dear Lord, to give us: YOUR holy faith (even more than we need to move those mountains, in JESUS' NAME!), the gift of praying in the Holy Spirit ("on earth, as it is in heaven"!), and YOUR never-ending mercy (which is new every morning! Great is YOUR faithfulness!)! Redeem, we pray – in the mighty, precious, and holy Name of

JESUS – ALL things that have come against these requests, with endtime ANOINTINGS in unlimited measure, such as this world has NEVER seen before! We soak this prayer in the BLOOD of Jesus, the HOLY anointing oil of the Holy Ghost, and the FIRE of God, in Jesus' Name! AMEN!

Matthew 24:9-14

9. Then you will be handed over to be persecuted and put to death, and you will be hated by all nations because of Me. 10. At that time many will turn away from the faith and will betray and hate each other, 11. and many false prophets will appear and deceive many people. 12. Because of the increase of wickedness, the love of most will grow cold, 13. but he who stands firm to the end will be saved. 14. And this gospel of the kingdom will be preached in the whole world as a testimony to all nations, and then the end will come.

Dear SOVEREIGN Lord of ALL creation, AUTHOR and FINISHER of our SALVATION, we HUMBLY come to YOU today with hearts OVERFLOWING with PRAISE to YOU – for Who YOU are and what YOU'VE done for us! YOU purchased us back from the grave with YOUR own life's BLOOD, JESUS, so that we can LIVE WITH YOU FOREVER! HALLELUIAH! YOU held back NOTHING from us but gave us YOUR VERY ALL! GLORY to YOUR HOLY, PRECIOUS, MIGHTY NAME, KING JESUS! YOU are WORTHY of our ALL!

Today we have a VERY special request: for YOU to use ALL of us, however YOU see fit, to bring the VERY MOST GLORY to YOU! We know that we are living in the end times, where persecution, martyrdom, betrayal, hate, deception, and lawlessness abound! YET we also know that YOU have a VERY specific plan for each of us, that only YOU can bring about! So we ask YOU, DEAR JESUS, to fully fulfill YOUR plan in us, so that YOU may be fully glorified through us! – for YOU are our all in ALL! We pour out our VERY LIVES to YOU, to be used as a DRINK OFFERING, oh God! Have YOUR HOLY, PERFECT WAY in us and through us – in JESUS' NAME – we pray. Redeem EVERYTHING in us that is not FULLY YIELDED to YOU (PAST, PRESENT, and FUTURE, PERMANENTLY and FOREVER) – in JESUS' holy, precious, mighty NAME – with endtime anointings in UNLIMITED measure, such as this world has NEVER seen before! We SOAK this prayer in the BLOOD of Jesus, the HOLY anointing oil of the Holy Ghost, and the FIRE of God, in JESUS' NAME. AMEN.

Exodus 14:24-25

24. During the last watch of the night the Lord looked down from the pillar of fire and cloud at the Egyptian army and threw it into confusion. 25. He made the wheels of their chariots come off so that they had difficulty driving. And the Egyptians said, "Let's get away from the Israelites! The Lord is fighting for them against Egypt."

Dear HOLY, PRECIOUS, and MIGHTY SAVIOR, we HUMBLY come to YOU today – to worship at YOUR holy feet, for YOU ALONE are WORTHY of ALL honor, praise, and majesty! YOU are exalted above the HIGHEST heaven! WORTHY are YOU, oh God of our salvation! YOU hold the universe in YOUR hand! Is ANYTHING too hard for YOU?!?

We cry out to YOU, dear Lord, to save us from our enemies! The battle has been long and hard, but we put our EVERLASTING trust in YOU, Who formed the earth out of NOTHING with YOUR words! HALLELUIAH! PRAISE Your holy, precious Name, for YOU are worthy of ALL honor, praise, and adoration! DELIVER us from those who plot evil against us! TROUBLE the army of the enemy, and REMOVE their chariot wheels – in the MIGHTY, MIGHTY, MIGHTY Name of JESUS! – so that they drive them with difficulty! SHOW them that YOU, the Lord God ALMIGHTY, are FIGHTING for us – in the NAME of Jesus Christ, SON of the Living God! – so that they TRY to flee in terror, but are CAUGHT in their own folly and EXPOSED to the LIGHT of LIGHTS! PLEASE redeem ALL evil that has EVER been directed against us (PAST, PRESENT, and FUTURE, PERMANENTLY and FOREVER), in the mighty and matchless Name of JESUS, King of kings and Lord of lords – with endtime anointings in unlimited measure, such as this world has NEVER seen before! We SOAK this prayer in the blood of Jesus, the holy anointing oil of the Holy Ghost, and the fire of God, in Jesus' Name. Amen.

Luke 24:46-49

46. He told them, "This is what is written: The Christ will suffer and rise from the dead on the third day, 47. and repentance and forgiveness of sins will be preached in His Name to all nations, beginning at Jerusalem. 48. You are witnesses of these things. 49. I am going to send you what My Father has promised; but stay in the city until you have been clothed with power from on high."

Dear HOLY and PRECIOUS Savior of ALL, we PRAISE YOUR holy and precious NAME – for YOU ALONE ARE WORTHY of our PRAISE! There is NONE like YOU in ALL the earth! HOLY, HOLY, HOLY are YOU, Lord God ALMIGHTY! The WHOLE earth is FULL of YOUR GLORY! PRAISE YOU, PRAISE YOU, PRAISE YOU in the HIGHEST! Let EVERYTHING that has breath, PRAISE the LORD! HALLELUIAH!

We HUMBLY come before YOUR PRESENCE with praise and thanksgiving to the KING of kings and the LORD of lords! We ask YOU now, dear LORD, to: send us to the nations, preaching repentance and remission of sins in YOUR NAME; send the Promise of YOUR FATHER upon us; and endue us with POWER from on high – in the precious, matchless, and holy NAME of JESUS! We HUMBLY ask YOU, dear LORD, to redeem ALL things that have come against these requests – in the mighty, matchless NAME of JESUS! – with endtime anointings in UNLIMITED measure, such as this world has NEVER seen before! We SOAK this prayer in the BLOOD of Jesus, the HOLY anointing oil of the HOLY GHOST, and the FIRE of God, in Jesus' Name. AMEN.

I Kings 18:26

26. So they took the bull given them and prepared it. Then they called on the name of Baal from morning till noon, "O Baal, answer us!" they shouted. But there was no response; no one answered. And they danced around the altar they had made.

Dear HOLY and PRECIOUS, MIGHTY God of ALL, we HUMBLY come before YOUR PRESENCE with THANKSGIVING and into YOUR COURTS with PRAISE! We MAGNIFY YOUR HOLY and PRECIOUS NAME, for YOU ALONE are WORTHY of ALL PRAISE, HONOR, and ADORATION! There is NONE like YOU in ALL THE EARTH! HOLY, HOLY, HOLY is YOUR PRECIOUS NAME! The WHOLE EARTH is FULL of YOUR GLORY! PRAISES to the KING of kings and the LORD of lords! HALLELUIAH!

We CALL upon YOU today, DEAR LORD, to HEAR our prayers! We are in DESPERATE NEED of YOU to ANSWER our prayers by YOUR HOLY FIRE! – for YOU ALONE are THE ONE, TRUE GOD of ALL! There is NO CONTEST! YOU HAVE ALREADY WON THE BATTLE! GO, GOD!!! We HUMBLE ourselves before YOUR

MIGHTY HAND, acknowledging that YOU ALONE are THE LORD GOD ALMIGHTY! We ask YOU, DEAR LORD, to SILENCE the voice of the enemy (PAST, PRESENT, and FUTURE, PERMANENTLY and FOREVER!) – in the HOLY, PRECIOUS, and MIGHTY NAME of JESUS! – so that he has NO VOICE AT ALL! PLEASE REDEEM ALL evil that has been thrown at us! – in the MIGHTY NAME of JESUS, KING of kings and LORD of lords! – for YOUR HONOR and YOUR GLORY (to make YOUR NAME KNOWN THROUGHOUT THE LAND!), with endtime anointings in UNLIMITED measure, such as this world has NEVER seen before! We SOAK this prayer in the BLOOD of Jesus, the HOLY anointing oil of the Holy Ghost, and the FIRE of God, in JESUS' NAME! AMEN!

Mark 13:5-8

5. Jesus said to them: "Watch out that no one deceives you. 6. Many will come in My Name, claiming, 'I am he,' and will deceive many. 7. When you hear of wars and rumors of wars, do not be alarmed. Such things must happen, but the end is still to come. 8. Nation will rise against nation, and kingdom against kingdom. There will be earthquakes in various places, and famines. These are the beginning of birth pains."

Dear GOD ALMIGHTY, LORD of heaven and earth, we HUMBLY come before YOU with THANKSGIVING in our hearts and PRAISES on our lips – EXALTING the PRECIOUS, HOLY, and MIGHTY NAME OF JESUS! YOU ALONE are WORTHY to be praised in ALL the earth! GREAT and MIGHTY is YOUR NAME in ALL THE EARTH! HOLY, HOLY, HOLY are YOU, oh LORD GOD ALMIGHTY! There is NONE like YOU in ALL THE EARTH! STRENGTH and MAJESTY are YOURS ALONE! ALL PRAISE and HONOR go to the KING of kings and the LORD of lords!

We HUMBLY come before YOUR holy throne, EXALTING YOU as LORD of ALL! YOU ALONE reign SUPREME in

ALL the earth! Let ALL the earth rejoice in CHRIST, her SAVIOR!

Dear Lord, we know that we are living in the "beginnings of sorrows" when we hear of "wars and rumors of wars" and "nation rising against nation, and kingdom against kingdom". We also know that "these things must happen", so we ask You now, dear Lord, to CAREFULLY watch over us and PROTECT us so that "NOONE deceives us" – in the holy, precious, and mighty NAME of JESUS! Keep our eyes WIDE OPEN to YOUR truth (PAST, PRESENT, and FUTURE, PERMANENTLY and FOREVER!) so that it is COMPLETELY and ABSOLUTELY IMPOSSIBLE to be led astray WHATSOEVER – in the NAME of JESUS, KING of kings and LORD of lords! – or to fall into ANY type of error (spirit, soul, or body)! Keep us SO RIVETED to YOU, JESUS, that we "are not troubled" in the slightest, "come what may" - for we KNOW (without a SHADOW of a doubt) WHOSE we are and WHO holds us securely (FOREVER!) in the palm of His hand! HALLELUIAH! We can NOT be shaken, for YOU are our ROCK and our SECURITY! ALL GLORY to YOUR precious, mighty NAME, for YOU ALONE are our PRAISE! Even though the earth be moved, we shall NOT be shaken! AMEN! Our trust is in YOU, and YOU ALONE – the LORD of heaven and earth!

We ask You, precious and holy, sovereign Savior of ALL, to REDEEM anything and everything that has come against these many requests – in the NAME of JESUS, for YOUR honor and YOUR glory – with endtime anointings in UNLIMITED measure, such as this world has NEVER seen before! We SOAK this prayer in the BLOOD of Jesus, the HOLY anointing oil of the Holy Ghost, and the FIRE of God, in JESUS' NAME! AMEN!

Esther 7:10-8:2

10. So they hanged Haman on the gallows he had prepared for Mordecai. Then the king's fury subsided. 8:1. That same day king Xerxes gave Queen Esther the estate of Haman, the enemy of the Jews. And Mordecai came into the presence of the king, for Esther had told how he was related to her. 2. The king took off his signet ring, which he had reclaimed from Haman, and presented it to Mordecai. And Esther appointed him over Haman's estate.

Dear GRACIOUS and BOUNTIFUL PROVIDER, BY Whom and FOR Whom ALL THINGS were created! – IN heaven, ON earth, and UNDER the earth! – we HUMBLY come before YOU with GRATEFUL HEARTS, acknowledging YOU as LORD of our lives! You ALONE are WORTHY of ALL PRAISE, HONOR, and ADORATION! There is NONE like YOU in ALL the earth! GLORY to YOUR HOLY, PRECIOUS NAME! We EXALT and LIFT YOU high, HIGHER than the HIGHEST HEAVEN, for YOU ALONE are WORTHY of our praise!

We HUMBLY approach YOUR throne of grace and mercy to request a favor from YOUR righteous, right hand, oh KING of the UNIVERSE! YOU KNOW that the enemy has stolen MUCH from us (SPIRIT, SOUL, and BODY); yet we also KNOW that YOU, oh KING who reigns FOREVERMORE, are in CONTROL and RICHLY REWARD those who put their trust in YOU! (There is NO OTHER GOD but YOU ALONE!) So we come to YOU, today, with THANKFUL HEARTS that we can put our COMPLETE and ABSOLUTE TRUST in YOU, SWEET JESUS! We ask YOU, oh HOLY ONE of ISRAEL, to COME TO OUR AID! DEFEND us and FIGHT for us as YOU did for Queen Esther so long ago, when YOU gave her the estate of her enemy (who was also the enemy of the Jews!)! REDEEM EVERY SINGLE THING that the enemy has EVER STOLEN from us (PAST, PRESENT, and FUTURE, PERMANENTLY and FOREVER!), with ENDTIME ANOINTINGS in UNLIMITED MEASURE, such as this world has NEVER SEEN BEFORE! We SOAK this prayer in the BLOOD of JESUS, the HOLY ANOINTING OIL of the HOLY GHOST, and the FIRE of GOD, in JESUS' NAME. AMEN.

Psalm 118:10-14

10. All the nations surrounded me, but in the Name of the Lord I cut them off. 11. They surrounded me on every side, but in the Name of the Lord I cut them off. 12. They swarmed around me like bees, but they died out as quickly as burning thorns; in the Name of the Lord I cut them off. 13. I was pushed back and about to fall, but the Lord helped me. 14. The Lord is my strength and my song; He has become my salvation.

Dear HOLY and PRECIOUS ONE of ISRAEL, YOU ALONE are WORTHY to be PRAISED! There is NONE like YOU in ALL the earth! GLORY to YOUR holy, precious, mighty Name, oh JEHOVAH! YOU are LORD of the NATIONS! NONE compares to YOU, oh Holy One of ISRAEL! YOU ARE the GREAT I AM; the BEGINNING and the END; the ONE WHO WAS, WHO IS, and WHO IS TO COME! AMEN!

Our ONLY desire, dear Lord, is to HONOR and EXALT YOUR HOLY, PRECIOUS, and MIGHTY NAME! YOU ARE the LORD of ALL! GLORY to the LORD of Hosts! HALLELUIAH!

As You know, we have been under HEAVY ATTACK by the enemy, lately! HOWEVER, we KNOW that YOU, oh God, are MUCH, MUCH, MUCH GREATER than ANYTHING or ANYBODY could EVER POSSIBLY BE (in this age AND in the one to come! AMEN!) When the enemy pushed me back, YOU, OH LORD GOD ALMIGHTY OF HEAVEN AND EARTH, kept me from falling! ALL PRAISE, HONOR, and GLORY belong to YOU, and YOU ALONE, oh GOD of the UNIVERSE!

When my enemies SURROUNDED me like bees, YOU, oh LORD GOD ALMIGHTY of heaven and earth, QUENCHED them like a fire of thorns! ALL PRAISE, HONOR, and GLORY belong to YOU, and YOU ALONE, oh PRECIOUS, SOVEREIGN LORD of ALL that exists! YOU have become my STRENGTH, my SONG, and my SALVATION! HOLY, HOLY, HOLY are YOU, oh LORD GOD ALMIGHTY! The WHOLE EARTH is FULL of YOUR GLORY! RIGHTEOUS and HOLY are ALL YOUR ways, oh SOVEREIGN LORD! We PRAISE YOUR MIGHTY NAME, for YOU ALONE are WORTHY! We GLORIFY YOUR MATCHLESS NAME, DEAR LORD!

Redeem EVERYTHING, we pray, that our enemies have even ATTEMPTED to send our way – in the PRECIOUS, HOLY, and MIGHTY, SOVEREIGN NAME of JESUS, KING of KINGS and LORD of LORDS! – with endtime anointings in UNLIMITED measure, such as this world has NEVER seen before! We SOAK this prayer in the BLOOD of JESUS, the HOLY anointing oil of the HOLY GHOST, and the FIRE of GOD, in JESUS' NAME! AMEN!

I Samuel 16:1

1. The Lord said to Samuel, "How long will you mourn for Saul, since I have rejected him as king over Israel? Fill your horn with oil and be on your way; I am sending you to Jesse of Bethlehem. I have chosen one of his sons to be king."

Dear Almighty and Sovereign Lord God of EVERYTHING, we EXALT and LIFT YOUR NAME on high, for YOU ALONE are WORTHY, oh LORD our GOD! We HUMBLY come before YOUR PRESENCE with thanksgiving and into YOUR COURTS with praise! We BLESS YOUR holy, precious NAME, for YOU ALONE are GOD of ALL! We MAGNIFY YOU, KING JESUS, and worship YOU ALONE! There is NONE like YOU in heaven or on earth! ALL praise belongs to YOU ALONE!

We understand that we are in a new season now. "Old things have passed away, and ALL THINGS have become new." So we DESIRE to MOVE WITH YOU, oh GOD! Where YOU lead, we will FOLLOW! We see that it is the time of "the changing of the guards". So just as You removed Saul from reigning over Israel as king and replaced him with King David (a man after God's own heart); so also, are YOU in the business, right now, of letting go of those in authority who are not leading "in step" with YOU, oh God! YOU have already provided their replacements, so that YOU can accomplish YOUR holy, perfect will "on earth, as it is in heaven"! We thank YOU and praise YOU for "cleaning house" so that YOU are free to move UNHINDERED throughout YOUR Church (YOUR Body!) during these end times! HALLELUIAH! ALL praise, honor, and glory belong to YOU, and YOU ALONE, oh holy one of Israel! "If YOU are for us, WHO can possibly, EVER be against us?!?" Though the earth be moved, WE shall NEVER, EVER, EVER be shaken; for our hope is in the LORD GOD ALMIGHTY, Who made heaven and earth! PRAISE YOU, PRAISE YOU, PRAISE YOU in the HIGHEST! Let EVERYTHING that has breath, PRAISE THE LORD! PRAISE YE THE LORD!

Our request, today, is simple: for YOU, dear Lord, to accomplish ALL of YOUR holy purposes! Remove ANYTHING and EVERYTHING that is NOT OF YOU, FOR YOU, and BY YOU – in the mighty, precious, and holy NAME of JESUS! – and replace them with YOUR holiness, YOUR purity, and YOUR cleanliness, we pray! Have YOUR COMPLETE and ABSOLUTE, PERFECT WAY IN ALL of us and THROUGH ALL of us, to bring about the most honor and glory to YOUR holy, precious, and mighty Name, Sweet Jesus! PLEASE REDEEM ALL BLOCKAGES that have prevented YOUR Holy Spirit from FULLY WORKING, MOVING, and MANIFESTING in YOUR CHURCH, THE BODY of JESUS CHRIST, our LORD and SAVIOR! – with endtime ANOINTINGS in UNLIMITED MEASURE, such as this world has NEVER seen before! We SOAK this prayer in the BLOOD of Jesus, the HOLY anointing oil of the Holy Ghost, and the FIRE of God, in Jesus' Name. Amen.

Isaiah 64:1-5a

1. Oh, that You would rend the heavens and come down, that the mountains would tremble before You! 2. As when fire sets twigs ablaze and causes water to boil, come down to make Your Name known to Your enemies and cause the nations to quake before You! 3. For when You did awesome things that we did not expect, You came down, and the mountains trembled before You. 4. Since ancient times no one has heard, no ear has perceived, no eye has seen any God besides You, who acts on behalf of those who wait for Him. 5. You come to the help of those who gladly do right, who remember Your ways.

Dear Lord God ALMIGHTY, MAKER of heaven and earth, to YOU ALONE do we worship and adore! There is NONE like YOU in ALL the earth! WORTHY is Your holy, precious, mighty NAME, oh Sovereign Lord God ALMIGHTY! We worship at YOUR holy feet and magnify YOUR holy NAME!

We ask YOU, dear Lord, to make YOUR presence known throughout the land! REND the heavens, oh MIGHTY

ONE, and display YOUR POWER for ALL to see! – even greater than YOU did so long ago (in the land of Egypt, when YOU delivered YOUR children from their captivity!)! Praise the LORD!

We know that YOU move MIGHTILY on behalf of those who wait for YOU, dear God. You reward those who rejoice in YOU, oh Lord God ALMIGHTY, and do righteousness! Just and holy are ALL Your ways, oh God our SAVIOR! The whole earth BOWS down to YOUR MAJESTY! So we are FULLY expecting You to do WONDERS in our day, such as this world has NEVER seen before, in JESUS' NAME! AMEN!

Please redeem ALL THINGS that have EVER, EVER, EVER prevented Your UNLIMITED, MIGHTY, and ALL-CONSUMING POWER from being FULLY and COMPLETELY manifest "on earth, as it is in heaven"! – in Jesus' holy, precious, and mighty Name we pray – with endtime anointings in UNLIMITED measure, such as this world has NEVER SEEN BEFORE! We SOAK this prayer in the blood of Jesus, the holy anointing oil of the Holy Ghost, and the fire of God, in JESUS' NAME! AMEN!

Ephesians 5:15-16

15. Be very careful, then, how you live – not as unwise but as wise, 16. making the most of every opportunity, because the days are evil.

Dear Lord God Almighty, Maker of heaven and earth, our PRECIOUS Redeemer, we HUMBLY come before YOUR PRESENCE with THANKSGIVING and into YOUR COURTS with PRAISE! We BLESS Your holy NAME, declaring YOU as Lord of all! HOLY, HOLY, HOLY are YOU, oh Lord God ALMIGHTY! ALL praise, honor, and glory belong to YOU ALONE, oh Majestic Creator of EVERYTHING!

We ask You, dear Lord, to help us to walk carefully, not as fools but as wise, redeeming the time, because the days are evil! ONLY YOU can help us navigate the way we need to go, through life! We FULLY rely upon YOU to lead and guide us on the right path, so that we will NOT be found foolish! We desire YOUR divine wisdom, oh GOD!

Redeem ALL foolishness in Your people (past, present, and future, permanently and forever!) – for YOUR holy, precious Name's sake – with endtime anointings in UNLIMITED measure, such as this world has never seen before! We soak this prayer in the blood of Jesus, the holy anointing oil of the Holy Ghost, and the fire of God, in Jesus' Name! Amen!

Judges 15:3-5

3. Samson said to them, "This time I have a right to get even with the Philistines; I will really harm them." 4. So he went out and caught three hundred foxes and tied them tail to tail in pairs. He then fastened a torch to every pair of tails, 5. lit the torches and let the foxes loose in the standing grain of the Philistines. He burned up the shocks and standing grain, together with the vineyards and olive groves.

Dear Awesome, Amazing, and All-Inspiring LORD GOD OF CREATION, we HUMBLY come before YOU today with HEARTS OVERFLOWING with PRAISE TO YOU! – for WHO YOU are and for WHAT YOU'VE DONE for us! NOBODY HAS EVER (or EVER WILL) done MORE or given up MORE than YOU have, SWEET JESUS, for us! PRAISE YOUR HOLY, PRECIOUS, MIGHTY NAME, JEHOVAH! We THANK YOU and PRAISE YOU from the VERY BOTTOM of our hearts! PRAISE YOU! PRAISE YOU! PRAISE YOU! PRAISE YOU!

We know, oh LORD, that YOU are a GOD OF JUSTICE, PERFECT and HOLY in ALL YOUR WAYS! GLORY to the

LORD of HOSTS! We THANK YOU that YOU ARE
BLAMELESS in ALL YOUR JUDGEMENTS – just as Samson
was when he burned the crops of the Philistines! So
when we see YOU destroying the "crops" of YOUR
enemies, we shall REJOICE that YOU are REIGNING
VICTORIOUS! – for vengeance TRULY IS THE LORD OF
HOSTS! We HUMBLY ask YOU, dear LORD, to REDEEM
ALL injustices in this world (past, present, and future,
permanently and forever!) – for YOUR holy, precious,
NAME'S SAKE, JESUS! – with endtime anointings in
UNLIMITED measure, such as this world has NEVER SEEN
BEFORE! We SOAK this prayer in the BLOOD of JESUS,
the HOLY anointing oil of the HOLY GHOST, and the
FIRE of GOD, in JESUS' NAME! AMEN!

Judges 6:11-12

11. The angel of the Lord came and sat down under the
oak in Ophrah that belonged to Joash the Abiezrite,
where his son Gideon was threshing wheat in a winepress
to keep it from the Midianites. 12. When the angel of the
Lord appeared to Gideon, he said, "The Lord is with you,
mighty warrior."

Dear Holy and Precious, MIGHTY God of ALL CREATION,
YOU are JUST and PERFECT in ALL YOUR WAYS! Holy,
holy, holy are YOU, oh LORD GOD ALMIGHTY! YOU are
FOR us as NOBODY else EVER COULD BE! HALLELUIAH!
YOU call us by name, and tell us that we belong to YOU!
Oh, GLORY! THANK YOU for Your unconditional love,
JESUS! THANK YOU for choosing us and promoting us
to sonship in YOUR ROYAL FAMILY, JESUS!

Just as YOU were with Gideon, so are YOU with us,
today! HALLELUIAH! When Gideon was hiding from the
Midianites, YOU found him and called him a "MIGHTY
WARRIOR"! PRAISE Your holy, precious NAME! Likewise,
with us, YOU found us and called us "mighty", because
that's what we are in YOU, JESUS! ALL THINGS TRULY

ARE POSSIBLE in CHRIST JESUS, OUR LORD! YOU specialize in taking the weak, hidden things of this world and turning them into STRONG, MIGHTY TOOLS to be used for Your Kingdom's purposes! GLORY to YOUR HOLY, PRECIOUS, MIGHTY NAME, KING JESUS! So THANK YOU for searching for us, finding us, and turning us into holy vessels fit for the KING'S SERVICE! AMEN!

We ask YOU, DEAR LORD, to PLEASE REDEEM ALL weakness and hiddenness in YOUR PEOPLE (YOUR FAMILY!) - in the MIGHTY, MIGHTY, MIGHTY NAME of JESUS CHRIST, LORD of HOSTS! – with endtime anointings in UNLIMITED measure, such as this world has NEVER SEEN BEFORE! We SOAK this prayer in the BLOOD of JESUS, the HOLY anointing oil of the HOLY GHOST, and the FIRE of GOD, in JESUS' NAME! AMEN!

Judges 5: 6-9

6. In the days of Shamgar son of Anath, in the days of Jael, the roads were abandoned; travelers took to winding paths. 7. Village life in Israel ceased, ceased until I, Deborah, arose, arose a mother in Israel. 8. When they chose new gods, war came to the city gates, and not a shield or spear was seen among forty thousand in Israel. 9. My heart is with Israel's princes, with the willing volunteers among the people. Praise the Lord!

Dear God Almighty, MAKER of heaven and earth, we BOW before YOUR holy throne, declaring YOU as LORD of ALL! There is NONE like our precious SAVIOR! HOLY and JUST are ALL YOUR WAYS, oh MIGHTY ONE of ISRAEL! YOU spoke, and the earth was formed, out of NOTHING! GLORY to Your holy NAME! GLORY! GLORY! GLORY!

We know, dear LORD, that YOU are an "ATMOSPHERE CHANGER", the VERY GREATEST there EVER WAS, IS, or WILL BE! GLORY to YOUR holy, precious, mighty NAME, oh JEHOVAH, LORD of HOSTS! Just as the roads were abandoned, and village life ceased in Israel until

DEBORAH arose to lead the people, so also does ALL life cease until GOD ALMIGHTY (LORD of heaven and earth and ALL that exists!) arises to lead HIS PEOPLE! HALLELUIAH!

In the days of Deborah, there was war, and the princes died with the people! ALL this happened because Israel chose new gods! They left their "FIRST LOVE" and suffered the consequences for it!

Dear LORD GOD ALMIGHTY, have MERCY upon us, we pray! BLOT out our iniquities for YOUR HOLY NAME'S SAKE! Remember our sins NO MORE! FORGIVE our trespasses, for against You, and YOU ONLY, have we SINNED! TURN our hearts back to YOU, oh LORD GOD, so that YOU are our LOVE, far FAR above ALL other loves COMBINED (in our lives)! We ask, DEAR LORD, that YOU teach us to love You as YOU love us! – wholly, completely, whole-heartedly, and UNCONDITIONALLY – with a love SO pure, SO holy, and SO bright, that the world will "KNOW we are CHRISTIANS, by our LOVE"! AMEN!

PLEASE "BLOW UP" our lives with YOUR HOLY,
UNQUENCHABLE PRESENCE! We want YOU, and ONLY
YOU, DEAR JESUS! We are HUNGRY and DESPERATE for
the "REAL THING"! NOTHING ELSE or NOTHING LESS
can (or EVER WILL) even COME CLOSE to satisfying!
EXPLODE upon the scene, here on PLANET EARTH, we
pray! DRAMATICALLY, DRASTICALLY, INSTANTLY, and
FOREVER change us – from GLORY to GLORY to GLORY!
– for YOUR honor and YOUR glory! AMEN!

We HUMBLY ask You, dear Lord, to REDEEM ALL dryness
and waywardness in our lives – for YOUR HONOR and
YOUR GLORY! – with endtime anointings in UNLIMITED
measure, such as this world has NEVER seen before! We
SOAK this prayer in the BLOOD of JESUS, the HOLY
anointing oil of the HOLY GHOST, and the FIRE of GOD,
in JESUS' NAME! AMEN!

Galatians 5:22-25

22. But the fruit of the Spirit is love, joy, peace, patience, kindness, goodness, faithfulness, 23. gentleness and self-control. Against such things there is no law. 24. Those who belong to Christ Jesus have crucified the sinful nature with its passions and desires. 25. Since we live by the Spirit, let us keep in step with the Spirit.

Dear Holy, Majestic, and SOVEREIGN Lord of ALL the Universe, we HUMBLY come before YOU, worshipping YOU as King SUPREME! There is NOONE like our God! YOU stand alone as the ONE and ONLY, TRUE GOD! HALLELUIAH to Your holy, precious, mighty NAME, oh JEHOVAH! We PRAISE You! We PRAISE You! We PRAISE You! We PRAISE You!

We know that there are nine fruits of the Spirit, Jesus; and since we live by the Spirit, we desire to keep in step with the Spirit! So we HUMBLY ask You, Christ Jesus, to crucify our sinful nature with its passions and desires! – for Your honor and Your glory! May we always be a sweet-smelling savor to You, Sweet Jesus! We desire to please You in every way possible! Your wish is our command!

Although there is NO law against these nine fruits, as we faithfully walk in the Spirit, we will experience YOUR true, unshakable, everlasting peace that transcends ALL understanding! Praise You for YOUR amazing goodness! You are WORTHY of all praise, honor, and adoration! Glory to Your holy, precious Name!

Please redeem ALL things that have prevented Your Holy Spirit's fruit from fully and completely manifesting in our lives! – with endtime anointings in UNLIMITED measure, such as this world has NEVER seen before! We SOAK this prayer in the blood of Jesus, the holy anointing oil of the Holy Ghost, and the fire of God, in Jesus' Name! Amen!

John 15:12-14

12. My command is this: Love each other as I have loved you. 13. Greater love has no one than this, that he lay down his life for his friends. 14. You are my friends if you do what I command.

Dear Holy and Mighty, Sovereign Savior of ALL, we HUMBLY worship You alone! There is NONE like You, Jesus! Holy and worthy is Your Name, oh GOD of the UNIVERSE! We BOW down before You, acknowledging YOU as Lord and Supreme Commander of EVERYTHING!

Thank You, Lord Jesus, for YOUR unconditional love, which caused You to lay down Your life for Your friends! We are eternally grateful for Your IMMENSE sacrifice of love! HALLELUIAH! Then, to top it off, You (The God of the UNIVERSE!) stoop to even call us Your friends! Wow! That is simply and completely mind-blowing!!! I am in complete awe and wonder of such an amazing God! GLORY to the King of kings! GLORY to the Lord of lords! "Love so amazing, so Divine, demands my soul, my life, my all!"

Our ONLY logical response to such a love as this, is to do as You command, which is to "love each other as You have loved us"! Noone ever, ever, ever has shown greater love than You did, Jesus – when You chose to pay the ultimate price for sinners such as us! When we were still in our sins, enemies of God, and "doing our own thing"; You, oh God (in Your infinite, everlasting, and tender mercy), reached down from heaven, pulled us out of the miry clay, and set our feet upon the Solid Rock (Jesus Christ!)! All I can say is, "Wow! Wow! And more WOW!" You simply and completely overwhelm me with Your amazing and infinite love! There is no one like my precious, precious Jesus! He is Lord of heaven and earth, and I will gladly and willingly follow Him until I die! AMEN!

We ask You, dear Lord, to love the world through us! Cause us to be Your "hands and feet"! Cause us to love, "as You first loved us"! – so that others will experience (first-hand) Your amazing, amazing love for them! HALLELUIAH! Redeem anything and everything that has ever, ever, ever prevented Your holy and perfect love from flowing (unhindered) through Your Church (Your Body!) to the world! – with endtime anointings in unlimited measure, such as this world has never seen before! We soak this prayer in the blood of Jesus, the holy anointing oil of the Holy Ghost, and the fire of God, in Jesus' Name. Amen.

Ephesians 4:25

25. Therefore each of you must put off falsehood and speak truthfully to his neighbor, for we are all members of one body.

Dear God Almighty, Lord of heaven and earth, we worship at Your holy throne, declaring You as Lord Supreme! There is none like You, Jesus, in heaven, on the earth, or under the earth! All glory, laud, and honor belong to You, and only You! Halleluiah!

Our prayer today, Jesus, is that we would put off falsehood and put on truth! – in the mighty, precious, and holy Name of Jesus! Our sole desire is to bring honor and glory to Your Name alone! May each of us speak truthfully to our neighbor, for we are all members of one Body! Halleluiah! May we look for opportunities to bless those with whom we come in contact!

Please redeem ALL falsehood in our lives (past, present, and future, permanently and forever) – for Your holy, precious Name's sake – with endtime anointings in

UNLIMITED measure, such as this world has NEVER seen before! We soak this prayer in the blood of Jesus, the holy anointing oil of the Holy Ghost, and the fire of God, in Jesus' Name. Amen.

Hebrews 11:17-19

17. By faith Abraham, when God tested him offered Isaac as a sacrifice. He who had received the promises was about to sacrifice his one and only son, 18. even though God had said to him, "It is through Isaac that your offspring will be reckoned." 19. Abraham reasoned that God could raise the dead, and figuratively speaking, he did receive Isaac back from death.

Dear Faithful, Faithful, Faithful God Almighty, we HUMBLY come before You with thanksgiving in our hearts and praises on our lips! YOU ALONE have never left us nor forsaken us, and YOU never will! It is not even a POSSIBILITY that You could ever forsake Your own BODY! (for we ARE the Body of Christ!)! HALLELUIAH! PRAISES to You, oh Mighty One – King of kings and Lord of lords!

Just as Abraham was found faithful before You, oh God, so also do we desire to be found faithful! When You tested Abraham, he willingly offered up Isaac, his one and only son! Abraham received the promises You gave

him, and he believed You with an unwavering faith!
PRAISE the Lord FOREVERMORE!

We offer ourselves up to YOU, oh Lord, as a LIVING
sacrifice! May we be found holy and acceptable to YOU,
dear Lord, through YOUR saving grace and
righteousness! Redeem EVERYTHING, we pray, that is
not found faithful to YOU, dear Lord! – with endtime
anointings in UNLIMITED measure, such as this world has
NEVER seen before! We soak this prayer in the BLOOD
of Jesus, the HOLY anointing oil of the Holy Ghost, and
the FIRE of God, in Jesus' Name! AMEN!

Ezra 8:21-23 & 31

21. There, by the Ahava Canal, I proclaimed a fast, so that we might humble ourselves before our God and ask Him for a safe journey for us and our children, with all our possessions. 22. I was ashamed to ask the king for soldiers and horsemen to protect us from enemies on the road, because we had told the king, "The gracious hand of our God is on everyone who looks to Him, but His great anger is against all who forsake Him." 23. So we fasted and petitioned our God about this, and He answered our prayer. 31. On the twelfth day of the first month we set out from the Ahava Canal to go to Jerusalem. The hand of our God was on us, and He protected us from enemies and bandits along the way.

Dear Lord God Almighty, we CRY out to YOU, for Your almighty PROTECTION from our enemies – for us and our CHILDREN, with all our POSSESSION! – in the mighty, precious, and holy NAME of JESUS, Lord of heaven and earth! "Though the earth be moved, we shall NOT be shaken, for our hope is in the Lord God Almighty, Who made the heavens and the earth!" HALLELUIAH!

Dear Lord God Almighty, we HUMBLY fast and petition YOU, for YOU to protect us from enemies on the "road of life"! – knowing (without a SHADOW of a doubt!) that You will ANSWER our prayers, for Your mercy's sake! HALLELUIAH!

As we HUMBLE ourselves before Your mighty hand, we fully know that we will not be ashamed before YOU, oh King of Creation! We have told everyone about the gracious hand of our God, which is on everyone who looks to HIM; but His great anger is against ALL who forsake Him!

PRAISE Your holy, precious, and mighty Name, oh JEHOVAH! You are worthy of all praise, honor, and adoration! The Lord God (Who leads Israel) neither slumbers nor sleeps! Therefore, "though the earth be moved, we shall not be shaken"! HALLELUIAH! All PRAISE and glory belong to YOU ALONE, dear Jesus! We HAIL You as King of our lives, oh JEHOVAH! Your "arm is not shortened that YOU cannot save"! All glory, laud, and honor belong to Christ, our King!

Just as You protected the returning Israelites during Ezra's time (when they set out to go to Jerusalem, on the twelfth day of the first month), so also will You protect us, from enemies and bandits along the way! No evil shall befall us! "Though we walk through the valley of the Shadow of Death, we will fear NO evil; for YOU are with us! YOUR rod and YOUR staff, they comfort us! YOU prepare a table before us in the presence of our enemies! YOU anoint our head with oil; our cup overflows! Surely goodness and mercy will follow us all the days of our life; and we shall dwell in the house of the Lord forever!" AMEN!

We petition You, oh holy One of Israel, to redeem all things that have ever, ever, EVER left us unprotected (spirit, soul, and body) or vulnerable to the attacks of the Evil One! – for Your Name's sake, JESUS! – with endtime anointings in UNLIMITED measure, such as this world has never seen before! We soak this prayer in the blood of Jesus, the holy anointing oil of the Holy Ghost, and the fire of God, in Jesus' Name. Amen.

Psalm 62:5

5. Find rest, O my soul, in God alone; my hope comes from Him.

Dear God Almighty, Maker of heaven and earth, our hearts are turned to You this day - in longing expectation for YOU ALONE, oh Holy One of Israel! Our soul finds rest in YOU ALONE! Our hope comes from You, oh Jehovah! "If God is for us, then who could ever, possibly be against us"?!?

Our God fights for us as nobody else can! HALLEUIAH! He is our Defender, Protector, and Shield! He is our EVERYTHING!

We ask You now, dear Lord God Almighty, to redeem all unrest and hopelessness in our lives (past, present, and future, permanently and forever) – for Your holy, precious Name's sake! – with endtime anointings in unlimited measure, such as this world has never seen before! We soak this prayer in the blood of Jesus, the holy anointing oil of the Holy Ghost, and the fire of God, in Jesus' Name! Amen!

Lamentations 3:25-27

25. The Lord is good to those whose hope is in Him, to the one who seeks Him; 26. it is good to wait quietly for the salvation of the Lord. 27. It is good for a man to bear the yoke while he is young.

Dear God of the Universe, we come to You, today, with hearts seeking HARD after You! We put our hope in YOU and wait quietly for YOUR salvation! We know that You are good to the one that does all these things! HALLELUIAH!

The Lord rewards the upright! "No good thing will He withhold from those that diligently seek His face!" Glory, glory, glory to the King of kings and the Lord of lords! All honor, praise, and adoration belong to You alone, oh Great and Mighty One!

We know that it is good for a man to bear the yoke while he is young! So we praise You that we have borne the yoke and come out of affliction stronger than ever before! HALLELUIAH! We have been refined in the fires

and are emerging as pure gold, fit for the King's service!
Only You could have taken such a mess as ourselves and
turned us into such gorgeous beauty, into which You can
pour Yourself and change the world (through us!)! Wow!
You are such an amazing, awesome God! We bow down
before You to give You all praise, honor, and glory that
befits the Kings of all kings! All praise, honor, and
majesty belong to You alone! Glory! Glory! Glory!

We HUMBLY ask You, dear Lord, to redeem all
impatience (on our part) as we quietly wait for You to
move (on our behalf), as only You can do! – with
endtime anointings in unlimited measure, such as this
world has never seen before! We soak this prayer in the
blood of Jesus, the holy anointing oil of the Holy Ghost,
and the fire of God, in Jesus' Name! Amen.

Daniel 6:24

24. At the king's command, the men who had falsely accused Daniel were brought in and thrown into the lions' den, along with their wives and children. And before they reached the floor of the den, the lions overpowered them and crushed all their bones.

Dear Lord God of heaven and earth, we worship at Your holy throne, declaring You as Lord of all! HALLELUIAH to the Sovereign One! You reign on high forevermore! There is none like You in heaven or on earth! Glory to the Lord of hosts! Strength and honor are Yours alone! We worship at Your holy feet and shout Your praises forevermore, oh Mighty, Holy, and Victorious One (in all the earth!)!

We have been falsely accused by our enemies, as You know! So we are asking You, dear Lord, to come to our aid as only You can! You fought for Daniel (in the lion's den) and kept the lions from eating him alive! HALLELUIAH! We know that "You are not a respecter of persons"! So we fully and simply trust that You will

defend us (as You did Daniel), when we call upon Your
Name! Glory in the Highest!

Daniel's enemies were all punished for speaking against
him! Even their children were overpowered by the lions!
So we ask for Your forgiveness and mercy for our
enemies, dear Lord! "They know not what they do!"
They have been under the devil's influence for so long,
that they think they are acting of their own accord! They
do not yet realize that they have been pawns, doing the
dirty work of the Evil One! Please open their eyes wide
to Your truth! Set them forever and completely free in
the mighty, precious, and holy Name of God Most High!

Please redeem all lies and false accusations targeted
against us (past, present, and future, permanently and
forever) – in the mighty, mighty, mighty Name of Jesus,
Lord of Hosts! – with endtime anointings in unlimited
measure, such as this world has never seen before! We
soak this prayer in the blood of Jesus, the holy anointing
oil of the Holy Ghost, and the fire of God, in Jesus' Name.
Amen.

Revelation 7:3-4

3. Do not harm the land or the sea or the trees until we put a seal on the foreheads of the servants of our God. 4. Then I heard the number of those who were sealed: 144,000 from all the tribes of Israel.

Dear God Almighty, Lord of heaven and earth and of all that exists, we humbly come before Your holy, majestic, and indescribable beauty! We are in complete awe of You and You alone! All glory to the King of kings and Lord of lords! There is none that compares to You – or even comes remotely close! AMEN!

We gratefully worship at Your holy throne, lifting You up higher and higher and higher! AMEN!

God Almighty, Maker of heaven and earth, we know that You have Your angels put a seal on the foreheads of the servants of God, prior to the coming judgments. This seal protects Your chosen people in the times ahead. Thank You for Your tender mercy, which is new every morning! Great is Your faithfulness to the children of men! HALLELUIAH!

We ask You, dear Lord, to seal us so completely (spirit, soul, and body, permanently and forever!) that all of the coming judgments simply pass over us and can't even touch us in any shape or form whatsoever! – in the precious, holy, and mighty Name of Jesus Christ, Lord of EVERYTHING! HALLELUIAH!

Please especially watch over Your chosen nation, Israel! Guard them, guide them, and protect them with Your unfailing love! Nurture them as a mother hen nurtures her young chicks! Be their Guardian, Defender, and Protector, in the mighty, holy, and precious Name of Jesus, Son of the LIVING GOD! AMEN!

Please redeem all things that have ever, ever left us unprotected and open to the attacks of the enemy (past, present, and future) – in the precious, holy, and mighty Name of God Most High! – with endtime anointings in UNLIMITED measure, such as this world has NEVER seen before! We soak this prayer in the blood of Jesus, the holy anointing oil of the Holy Ghost, and the fire of God, in Jesus' Name! AMEN!

Judges 3:29-30

29. At that time they struck down about ten thousand Moabites, all vigorous and strong; not a man escaped. 30. That day Moab was made subject to Israel, and the land had peace for eighty years.

Dear God Almighty, Lord of heaven and earth, Maker of the UNIVERSE, You are our absolute EVERYTHING! Nothing exists without You! We can't even breathe on our own, unless YOU, oh Lord of all, give us our next breath! HALLELUIAH! All glory to Your holy, precious, mighty Name! You alone are worthy of all of our praise, honor, and adoration! We give no glory to any other, but to You alone, Sweet JESUS!

Dear Lord God Almighty, we fall on our faces before YOU to worship the KING, Who reigns forevermore! Glory, glory, glory to Him Who sits on the throne and reigns on HIGH!

We know, dear Lord, that YOU fought for the Israelites – time and time and time again! In the book of Judges,

YOU struck down about ten thousand Moabites, all vigorous and strong – so that not even one man escaped! HALLELUIAH! All glory to Your holy, precious, mighty NAME! (Who can ever, possibly stand before YOU, oh Mighty One of Israel?!?) That day Moab was made subject to Israel, and the land had peace for eighty years!!!

We HUMBLY ask You to fight for us, as You did for the Israelites so long ago! SMITE down Your enemies with VENGEANCE, we pray! May YOUR fame spread throughout the earth like a massive, massive, MASSIVE tidal wave! – so that all nations, peoples, tribes, and tongues will hear (and speak) of YOUR Great Name! HALLELUIAH! HALLEUIAH! HALLELUIAH!

Please redeem ALL honor and glory that have ever, ever, EVER been stolen from You, oh God Most HIGH! – past, present, and future, permanently and FOREVER! – with endtime anointings in unlimited measure, such as this world has NEVER seen before! We soak this prayer in the BLOOD of Jesus, the HOLY anointing oil of the Holy Ghost, and the FIRE of God, in Jesus' Name! AMEN!

Proverbs 3:34-35

34. He mocks proud mockers but gives grace to the humble. 35. The wise inherit honor, but fools He holds up to shame.

Dear Lord God ALMIGHTY, we come before YOUR PRESENCE with thanksgiving and into YOUR COURTS with praise! We thank and bless YOUR holy, precious, mighty NAME; for YOU ALONE are highly exalted, far above ALL other names combined! HALLELUIAH!

"The mountains and the hills will break forth before YOU, and all the trees of the field will clap their hands!"

We honor and exalt the Lord God Almighty, Maker of heaven and earth – the Eternal One Who reigns on high forevermore! HALLELUIAH! Praise His holy, precious, and mighty Name! Let all the earth rejoice in Christ her Savior! AMEN!

We know, dear Lord, that YOU mock the proud mockers but give grace to the humble! PRAISE You, Jesus, for YOUR holy, perfect, and matchless ways! Who can know or understand them?!?

We also know that the wise inherit honor, but fools are held up to shame! So we humbly ask YOU, dear Lord, to bestow upon us the full humbleness and wisdom of Jesus Christ Himself, in the mighty, precious, and holy Name of Jesus! AMEN!

Please redeem all things that have ever, ever, EVER come against Your humbleness and wisdom from being poured into Your Body! (the Church of Jesus Christ Himself!)! – with endtime anointings in UNLIMITED measure, such as this world has never seen before! We SOAK this prayer in the blood of Jesus, the holy anointing oil of the Holy Ghost, and the fire of God, in Jesus' Name! AMEN!

Amos 3:14-15

14."On the day I punish Israel for her sins, I will destroy the altars of Bethel; the horns of the altar will be cut off and fall to the ground. 15. I will tear down the winter house along with the summer house; the houses adorned with ivory will be destroyed and the mansions will be demolished," declares the Lord.

Dear Almighty and Sovereign Lord, there is none like YOU in heaven, or on earth, or under the earth! All glory to Your holy, matchless NAME, oh JEHOVAH! The earth is FULL of YOUR GLORY! PRAISES to the King of all kings!

We know that when You punished Israel for her sins, You destroyed the altars of Bethel so that the horns of the altar were cut off and fell to the ground! GLORY to Your holy, precious, and mighty Name, Sweet JESUS!

You also tore down the winter house along with the summer house! The houses adorned with ivory were destroyed, and the mansions were demolished! PRAISE the Lord forevermore! PRAISE Him in the Highest! "Let everything that has breath, praise ye the LORD!" HALLELUIAH!

You, oh Lord, are the MIGHTY ONE, dressed for battle! YOU ALONE are arrayed in fine splendor and ready to cleanse the land of all of its impurities, contaminations, and blemishes! HALLELUIAH! All glory to the "Redeemer of Israel", Who fully purges the earth of her sins and iniquities! – in order to bring "heaven on earth"! (There must be a thorough cleansing before God can bring about His Kingdom purposes, here on earth, "as it is in heaven"!)

So we HUMBLY ask You, Sweet Jesus, to please tear down anything and everything in our lives that is at all offensive to Your Holy Spirit! (past, present, and future, PERMANENTLY and FOREVER!)! – in the MIGHTY, MIGHTY, MIGHTY Name of JESUS, COMMANDER of the ANGELIC ARMIES! HALLELUIAH!

Please REDEEM ALL of our offenses! ("Against You, and YOU ONLY, have we sinned and done this evil in Your sight!") – with endtime anointings in UNLIMITED measure, such as this world has never seen before! We SOAK this prayer in the blood of Jesus, the holy anointing oil of the Holy Ghost, and the fire of God, in Jesus' Name! AMEN!

Luke 5:33-34

33.They said to Him, "John's disciples often fast and pray, and so do the disciples of the Pharisees, but Yours go on eating and drinking." 34. Jesus answered, "Can you make the guests of the bridegroom fast while He is with them?"

Dear Lord God of ALL creation, GLORY to YOUR holy, precious NAME, oh JEHOVAH! We worship YOU above ALL others and claim YOU as our KING! All praise and honor belong to YOU ALONE, for YOU are worthy of our very, very ALL!

We know, oh Lord, that (in the book of Luke) both the disciples of John and of the Pharisees often fasted and prayed. Meanwhile, Jesus' disciples continued on eating and drinking.

Jesus' disciples could not fast, because you can't make the guests of the Bridegroom fast while He is with them! However, when Jesus was taken from them, then they fasted! Likewise, for us, the time to fast is NOW! We should be seeking God's face with EARNEST prayers and fastings, for these are PERILOUS TIMES in which we live! These times are not for the faint-hearted, but "our hope is in the Lord God Almighty Who made heaven and earth! He shall not allow our foot to be moved! He Who keeps Israel, neither slumbers nor sleeps!"

So we HUMBLY ask You, dear and precious Savior, to teach us how to pray and fast as Jesus did (while He was on earth)! We need to learn from our Master, the very best Example and Teacher there EVER was! – so that we will be fully armed and dangerous to the enemy in these Last Days!

Please redeem ALL spiritual laziness and apathy (in our lives)! – past, present, and future, permanently and FOREVER! – with endtime anointings in UNLIMITED measure, such as this world has NEVER SEEN BEFORE! We SOAK this prayer in the BLOOD of Jesus, the HOLY anointing oil of the Holy Ghost, and the FIRE of God, in JESUS' NAME! AMEN!

John 5:43-46

43. I have come in My Father's Name, and you do not accept Me; but if someone else comes in his own name, you will accept him. 44. How can you believe if you accept praise from one another, yet make no effort to obtain the praise that comes from the only God? 45. But do not think I will accuse you before the Father. Your accuser is Moses, on whom your hopes are set. 46. If you believed Moses, you would believe Me, for he wrote about Me.

Dear Holy and Heavenly Father, Lord God of ALL creation, we HUMBLY come before You, today, to worship YOU above the highest heaven! There is NONE like You, dear Jesus! Nobody or nothing even remotely comes close to comparing to YOU! – in majesty, splendor, power, glory, might, and in every other amazing, imaginable way! HALLELUIAH! All glory to the King of all kings!

We know, Precious Savior, that YOU came (to the earth) in Your Father's Name; yet You said, "You do not accept Me. How can you believe if you accept praise from one another, yet make no effort to obtain the praise that comes from the only God?"

The people in Jesus' time did not think that He would accuse them before the Father. They didn't realize that their accuser was Moses, on whom their hopes were set!

So we HUMBLY ask You, dear and precious Savior, to open our eyes WIDE to what is going on all around us! May we NOT be like "ostriches that have their head stuck in the sand"! We DESIRE to be constantly aware of what YOU are doing and where YOU are moving! HALLELUIAH! We definitely do NOT want to miss out on the coming move of God, as many of the people did during Jesus' time here on earth!

We so very, very, VERY desperately want to move WITH YOU, oh God! We want to "keep in step with You", dear Lord God ALMIGHTY! "Where You go, we will gladly and willingly follow!" Praises to the Lord of Hosts! Praises to the King of kings!

We HUMBLY ask You now, oh holy and righteous God, to redeem anything and everything that has ever been "out of step" with moving with You (past, present, and future, permanently and FOREVER!), with endtime ANOINTINGS in UNLIMITED measure, such as this world has never seen before! We SOAK this prayer in the blood of Jesus, the hoy anointing oil of the Holy Ghost, and the fire of God, in Jesus' Name. AMEN!

II Corinthians 5:21

21. God made Him who had no sin to be sin for us, so that in Him we might become the righteousness of God.

Dear Holy and Awesome God of all the Universe, how majestic is Your Name in all the earth! It is for Your glory that we were created! Halleluiah! May we live every moment of every day for that express purpose, and that alone! – to give all honor and glory to our Creator who continues to sustain us! Glory! Glory! Glory!

All hail to King Jesus, who saves us from our sins! You freely paid the ultimate price, in order to eternally reconcile us to Your Father God and to set us free from the power of sin forever and ever and ever! AMEN! HALLELUIAH! All glory to the Prince of Peace!

We HUMBLY thank You, dear Jesus, for paying the penalty for sin, which is death! Through You, we might become the righteousness of God! HALLELUIAH! "Glory to God in the Highest, and on earth, peace and good will toward men, on whom His favor rests!" WOW! "Love so

amazing, so Divine, demands my soul, my life, my all!"
HALLELUIAH!

Our hearts are simply EXPLODING with pure and simple gratitude to You, Jesus, for such an amazing, selfless, and perfect love! May we always love as You love, give as You give, and do as You do – in thought, word, and deed – all the days of our lives! Glory! Glory! Glory!

Please redeem all lack of thankfulness in our lives – past, present, and future, permanently and forever! – with endtime ANOINTINGS in UNLIMITED MEASURE, such as this world has NEVER SEEN BEFORE! We soak this prayer in the blood of Jesus, the holy anointing oil of the Holy Ghost, and the fire of God, in Jesus' Name. AMEN!

I Corinthians 5:12-13

12. What business is it of mine to judge those outside the church? Are you not to judge those inside? 13. God will judge those outside. "Expel the wicked man from among you."

Dear Lord God of ALL the earth, WORTHY is Your holy, precious NAME! We EXALT and lift You high – higher and higher and higher and HIGHER! AMEN!

There is NONE like You in ALL the earth! WORTHY are YOU, oh Lord God Almighty! STRENGTH and HONOR and MAJESTY are YOURS ALONE! You hold the WHOLE WORLD in Your hands! HALLELUIAH! Glory to the MIGHTY ONE, Who reigns on high forevermore! AMEN!

We know, oh Lord, that YOU are the God who judges ALL MEN! NOBODY escapes Your scrutiny! HALLELLUIAH! We praise You for YOUR JUSTICE! When we see the wicked prospering (while the godly are struggling), it often oppresses us until..."I entered the sanctuary of God; then I understood their final destiny"!

In the end, oh God, You really do make all things right! Glory to Your holy, mighty Name, JESUS!

We see (in I Corinthians) that it is the business of the Church to judge ONLY those inside of the Church. It is GOD'S business to judge those outside!

The Church is commanded to EXPEL the wicked man, so that he will NOT CONTAMINATE the WHOLE CHURCH! We can NOT afford (in these last days) to "let a little yeast work through the whole batch of dough! We MUST get rid of the old yeast, so that we may be a new batch without yeast!"

Although this is not a popular topic with churches that are trying to fill their seats, it is DEFINITELY a Scriptural one! So we choose to OBEY Your holy Word, dear God, and keep our churches as "clean" as possible! In order to do this, dear Lord, we NEED Your help! We HUMBLY ask You for Your direction, Your insight, and Your wisdom in handling this situation! We can NOT do it without You!

Thank You for leading us each step of the way! Redeem ALL wickedness that has infiltrated our churches, we pray, for Your Name's sake! – with endtime anointings in UNLIMITED measure, such as this world has NEVER seen before! We soak this prayer in the blood of Jesus, the holy anointing oil of the Holy Ghost, and the fire of God, in Jesus' Name! AMEN!

I Samuel 7:13-14

13. So the Philistines were subdued and did not invade Israelite territory again. Throughout Samuel's lifetime, the hand of the Lord was against the Philistines. 14. The towns from Ekron to Gath that the Philistines had captured from Israel were restored to her, and Israel delivered the neighboring territory from the power of the Philistines. And there was peace between Israel and the Amorites.

Dear Holy and Precious Savior, YOU are worthy of ALL honor, praise, and glory! HALLELUIAH! We LOVE YOU, Sweet Jesus, and BOW DOWN before YOU, giving honor where honor is due!

In I Samuel, we see that the Philistines were subdued and did not invade Israelite territory again! In fact, throughout Samuel's lifetime, the hand of the Lord was against the Philistines! Israel even delivered the neighboring territory from the power of the Philistines, and there was peace between Israel and the Amorites!

So we see, here, that You, oh God, fought for Israel against her enemies! HALLELUIAH! There is NO GOD like our God! You ALONE reign Supreme! PRAISE Your holy, precious Name, oh MIGHTY JEHOVAH who does wonders beyond our COMPREHENSION! WORTHY, WORHTY, WORTHY are You, oh King who REIGNS on high!

We HUMBLY ask You now, dear Jesus, to FIGHT for us as You did for Your chosen nation, Israel! DELIVER us from our enemies, so that we live at peace with our neighbors all of our lives! AMEN!

Please REDEEM all unrest in our lives (past, present, and future, permanently and forever!) with endtime ANOINTINGS in UNLIMITED MEASURE, such as this world has NEVER SEEN BEFORE! We SOAK this prayer in the BLOOD of Jesus, the HOLY anointing oil of the Holy Ghost, and the FIRE of God, in Jesus' Name. AMEN!

I Kings 7:51

51.When all the work King Solomon had done for the temple of the Lord was finished, he brought in the things his father David had dedicated – the silver and gold and the furnishings – and he placed them in the treasuries of the Lord's temple.

Dear Holy and Sovereign God, we WORSHIP at Your holy feet, declaring You as Lord of all! There is NONE like our precious Savior who reigns in majesty!

We see that Solomon brought in the things his father David had dedicated, and he placed them in the treasuries of the Lord's temple because he was finished.

Solomon did as the Lord instructed him. He was used to build the Lord's temple, thereby bringing honor and glory to God Most High! HALLELUIAH!

May we always be Your willing vessels, Jesus! – fit for our Master's service! May our lives be examples of radical, yielded, and laid-down obedience to You, oh Sovereign King Victorious! Let us desire the things that You desire, so that our hearts will beat as one! Whatever Your assignment is for us in life, may we fulfill it wholeheartedly "as unto the Lord"! Amen!

Please redeem all negligence and outright disobedience (on our part) – past, present, and future, permanently and forever – with endtime anointings in unlimited measure, such as this world has never seen before! We soak this prayer in the blood of Jesus, the holy anointing oil of the Holy Ghost, and the fire of God, in Jesus' Name! Amen!

Deuteronomy 3:27-28

27. Go up to the top of Pisgah and look west and north and south and east. Look at the land with your own eyes, since you are not going to cross this Jordan. 28. But commission Joshua, and encourage and strengthen him, for he will lead this people across and will cause them to inherit the land that you will see.

Dear Lord God of heaven and earth, the whole earth is full of Your glory! Worthy is Your precious name, oh Jehovah! There is none like You! We praise You, oh Holy One of Israel!

Lord, You told Moses that he would not cross the Jordan River. However, You instructed him to encourage Joshua, as he would lead the Israelites across the Jordan River to inherit the Promised Land! What an absolutely glorious day it must have been for Israel, when they finally entered the land that had been promised to them for generations! Glory to God in the HIGHEST!

Our prayer request today, Sweet Jesus, is to humbly ask You to CATAPULT us into our Promised Land! The journey has been long and treacherous, but You, oh Merciful God, have sustained us and carried us safely through the Wilderness! HALLELUIAH!

Thank You for Your tender mercies and loving care along the way! We literally could not have made it without You! The enemy tried (many times) to take us out, but You, oh Lord God Almighty of heaven and earth, fought for us! You had our backs as noone else did! HALLELUIAH! All glory to the King Eternal who reigns FOREVERMORE!

We HUMBLY ask You now, dear Jesus, to redeem anything and everything that has ever, ever, EVER prevented us from crossing our Jordan River and moving into our Promised Land! – with endtime anointings in UNLIMITED measure, such as this world has NEVER SEEN BEFORE! We SOAK this prayer in the BLOOD of Jesus, the HOLY anointing oil of the Holy Ghost, and the FIRE of God, in JESUS' NAME. AMEN!

John 3:29-30

29. The bride belongs to the bridegroom. The friend who attends the bridegroom waits and listens for him, and is full of joy when he hears the bridegroom's voice. That joy is mine, and it is now complete. 30. He must become greater; I must become less.

Dear Almighty Lord God of all things, we HUMBLY come before You with pure and simple joy! We are the Bride of Christ and anxiously await our Bridegroom's arrival! We KNOW that Your return, Jesus, is very, very, VERY soon! HALLELUIAH!

Just as John the Baptist listened and heard Your voice, Jesus, so also are we listening for You! We SO desire to hear Your sweet voice! That joy is mine when I know that You are almost here! I have been waiting my whole life to see You face to face! Now that You are almost here, I can HARDLY WAIT! Oh what JOY shall fill my heart! GLORY! GLORY! HALLELUIAH!

Our desire, Jesus, is for You to become GREATER and for us to become LESS! You must INCREASE while we DECREASE! That is the only way to truly bring "heaven on earth"!

Our request today is simple: Jesus, please magnify Yourself through us, we pray! Let the world see YOU when they look at us! May we be SO FILLED (to OVERFLOWING!) with YOU, JESUS, that the world sees YOU, and ONLY YOU, when they encounter us! We want people to be drawn to YOU, like magnets! The time is short, and so there is much to be done! It is HARVEST TIME! OH, GLORY! The GREATEST TIME IN ALL OF HISTORY is ALMOST HERE, and we get to be a part of it! HALLELUIAH!

Please redeem anything and everything that has ever kept people from seeing YOU, JESUS, in our lives, we pray! – with endtime ANOINTINGS in UNLIMITED MEASURE, such as this world has never seen before! We SOAK this prayer in the BLOOD of Jesus, the HOLY anointing oil of the Holy Ghost, and the FIRE of God, in JESUS' NAME! AMEN!

II Samuel 3:35-36

35. Then they all came and urged David to eat something while it was still day; but David took an oath, saying, "May God deal with me, be it ever so severely, if I taste bread or anything else before the sun sets!" 36. All the people took note and were pleased; indeed, everything the king did pleased them.

Dear Lord God Almighty, Maker of heaven and earth, we bow low before You to PROCLAIM You as our King – the ONE and ONLY! HALLELUIAH!

Just as King David took an oath and refused to eat something – in honor of Abner, who had died - so also should we honor You, King Jesus, in ALL that we do! If David could honor a mere mortal like that, how much more should we honor the King of all kings and the Lord of all lords – who lives forevermore! AMEN!

We HUMBLY ask You, dear Jesus, to teach us to honor You as You deserve to be honored! May our every thought, word, and deed glorify You COMPLETELY, we pray! We were created to GLORIFY You and ENJOY You forever! AMEN!

We see that everything that the king did pleased the people. He was an exceptional king in reigning over them. Of course, he was NOTHING compared to You, KING JESUS! You STAND ALONE in BEAUTY, MAJESTY, and POWER!

Please teach me Your ways, oh God, so that I may walk in them and be pleasing to You! May I be a sweet-smelling savor to You as I live my life for YOUR GLORY ALONE! HALLELUIAH!

Please redeem ALL things that have EVER, EVER not brought FULL honor to YOU ALONE, Sweet Jesus! – with ENDTIME ANOINTINGS in UNLIMITED MEASURE, such as this world has NEVER SEEN BEFORE! We SOAK this prayer in the BLOOD of Jesus, the HOLY anointing oil of the Holy Ghost, and the FIRE of God, in JESUS' NAME! AMEN!

Job 12:4-5

4. I have become a laughingstock to my friends, though I called upon God and He answered – a mere laughingstock, though righteous and blameless! 5. Men at ease have contempt for misfortune as the fate of those whose feet are slipping.

Dearest Holy One of Israel, YOU are worthy of ALL our praise, worship, and adoration! HOLY, HOLY, HOLY are You, oh Lord God ALMIGHTY! The whole earth is FULL of Your glory! Praises to the KING of all kings!

Job felt that he had become a mere laughingstock to his friends, even though he had called upon God. He felt as if his feet were slipping!

Of course, we know the ending of the story where God Almighty shows up in a very huge way! Then God "prospered Job and gave him twice as much as he had before...even blessing him with seven sons and three daughters"! HALLELUIAH!

Dear God, You see what we have had to endure at the hands of the enemy. HOWEVER, we KNOW (without a SHADOW of a doubt!) that You GREATLY reward those "that put their trust in YOU"! So we are trusting YOU COMPLETELY, knowing that YOU have our best interests at heart and will work ALL things together for our good and YOUR GLORY! HALLELUIAH!

So we ask You now, PRECIOUS SAVIOR, to bless us IMMEASURABLY! – as only YOU CAN! Redeem ALL things that the enemy has stolen from us – past, present, and future, permanently and FOREVER! – with endtime ANOINTINGS in UNLIMITED MEASURE, such as this world has NEVER SEEN BEFORE! We SOAK this prayer in the BLOOD of Jesus, the HOLY anointing oil of the Holy Ghost, and the FIRE of God, in Jesus' Name! AMEN!

Psalm 71:9-12

9. Do not cast me away when I am old; do not forsake me when my strength is gone. 10. For my enemies speak against me; those who wait to kill me conspire together. 11. They say, "God has forsaken him; pursue him and seize him, for no one will rescue him." 12. Be not far from me, O God; come quickly, O my God, to help me.

Dear Holy and Mighty God of ALL Creation, WORTHY is Your precious Name! There is NONE like YOU in ALL the earth! MIGHTY, MIGHTY, MIGHTY are YOU, oh God of ALL!

The psalmist is despondent (in this passage). He feels that his enemies speak against him and wait to kill him! They conspire together!

Our humble prayer request today is (like the psalmist): that You, oh God, would not be far from us! Come QUICKLY to help us! There is none like You that can defend, fight, and protect! HALLELUIAH!

Please redeem all things that have ever, ever, EVER been spoken against us, conspired against us, and done against us (in the precious, mighty and holy Name of Jesus Christ, Son of the LIVING GOD!) – past, present, and future, PERMANENTLY and FOREVER! – with endtime ANOINTINGS in UNLIMITED MEASURE, such as this world has NEVER SEEN BEFORE! We SOAK this prayer in the BLOOD of Jesus, the HOLY anointing oil of the Holy Ghost, and the FIRE of God, in JESUS' NAME. AMEN!

Ecclesiastes 12:1

1. Remember your Creator in the days of your youth, before the days of trouble come and the years approach when you will say, "I find no pleasure in them."

Dear Holy, Precious God of ALL Creation, WORTHY is Your NAME in ALL THE EARTH! Holy, holy, holy are YOU, oh Lord God Almighty! The whole earth is FILLED with Your glory! Praises to the KING of all kings! Glory! Glory! Glory!

Dear Lord God of heaven and earth, we HUMBLY come to You today to remember our Creator! – the very One "who formed us while we were still in our mother's womb"! GLORY to God Almighty! We TRULY are "fearfully and wonderfully made"! You even know the number of hairs on our head! There is no one who knows us as intimately as You do, dear Jesus! HALLELUIAH!

Thank You for loving us and caring for us as You do! There is NO love like our Heavenly Father's love! YOU love us DEEPER than the DEEPEST ocean with a love that NEVER runs dry! HALLELUIAH! May we love YOU like that and live our lives SO COMPLETELY for You, Sweet Jesus, in the days of our youth! May we give You the BEST years of our lives while life is still worth living! GLORY to our God who reigns on high FOREVERMORE! AMEN!

Please redeem all the years that the locusts have eaten! (for Your precious, holy, and mighty Name's sake, Jesus!) – past, present, and future, permanently and FOREVER! – with endtime anointings in unlimited measure, such as this world has never seen before! We soak this prayer in the blood of Jesus, the holy anointing oil of the Holy Ghost, and the fire of God, in Jesus' Name. Amen!

Song of Solomon 2:11-13

11. See! The winter is past; the rains are over and gone.
12. Flowers appear on the earth; the season of singing has come, the cooing of doves is heard in our land. 13. The fig tree forms its early fruit; the blossoming vines spread their fragrance. Arise, come, my darling; my beautiful one, come with me.

Dear Lord God in the HIGHEST, WORHTY is Your Name in ALL the earth! YOU ALONE are: "The Great I Am", "The Beginning and the End", "The Alpha and the Omega"! There is NONE like our Great and Mighty JEHOVAH! AWESOME and JUST are ALL Your ways, oh HOLY ONE of ISRAEL!

We are simply HUMBLED by Your AMAZING GOODNESS to us, Precious, Heavenly Father! We are in COMPLETE AWE of HOW MUCH You love us and take care of us! HALLELUIAH! GLORY to Your holy, precious, mighty Name, SWEET JESUS! There is NONE like You in heaven, or on the earth, or under the earth! All glory, praise, and honor belong to YOU ALONE, KING JESUS!

Thank You for carrying us safely through the winter! We are SO GRATEFUL that the rains are over and gone! HALLELUIAH! The old season is past, and the new season has JUST BEGUN! Glory! Glory! Glory!

We HUMBLY ask You now, dear Jesus, to cause us to "bloom where planted"! May we blossom (in ALL THINGS) for the glory of God HIMSELF! We desire NO GLORY for ourselves but want (ABOVE ALL ELSE!) to bring YOU all HONOR, PRAISE, and GLORY that befits the KING of all kings! HALLELUIAH!

Please redeem ALL THINGS (in our lives) that have ever been dead, dry or wilted – past, present, and future, permanently and FOREVER! – with endtime ANOINTINGS in UNLIMITED measure, such as this world has NEVER SEEN BEFORE! We SOAK this prayer in the BLOOD of Jesus, the HOLY anointing oil of the Holy Ghost, and the FIRE of God, in JESUS' NAME! AMEN!

Zechariah 1:2-6

2. The Lord was very angry with your forefathers. 3. Therefore tell the people: This is what the Lord Almighty says: "Return to Me," declares the Lord Almighty, "and I will return to you," says the Lord Almighty. 4. Do not be like your forefathers, to whom the earlier prophets proclaimed: This is what the Lord Almighty says: "Turn from your evil ways and your evil practices." But they would not listen or pay attention to Me, declares the Lord. 5. Where are your forefathers now? And the prophets, do they live forever? 6. But did not My words and My decrees, which I commanded My servants the prophets, overtake your forefathers?

Dear Holy, Mighty, and Sovereign Savior of ALL, we HUMBLY come before You with grateful hearts! There is NONE like You in ALL the earth! WORTHY is Your holy, precious Name, oh JEHOVAH, KING of kings and LORD of lords!

In Zechariah, we see that YOU, oh Lord God Almighty, were VERY ANGRY with the Israelite's forefathers. They would NOT listen to Your prophets and TURN from their

EVIL WAYS! As a result, the warnings that YOU gave them (through Your prophets) came to pass! It was only THEN that they repented!

Oh, DEAR LORD GOD of HEAVEN and EARTH, PLEASE don't let that happen to us! Have MERCY upon us, we pray! WAKE us up before it is TOO LATE, and You are left with NO CHOICE but to KEEP YOUR WORD and rain down Your JUST JUDGMENTS upon us! – for YOU are a holy God that DETESTS sin and iniquity!

When You punish people, it is ONLY as a LAST RESORT! You ALWAYS try "the disciplining approach" FIRST to get our attention! If THAT doesn't work (after repeated attempts on Your part), then You MUST intervene out of NECESSITY! – in order to RESCUE mankind from DESTROYING HIMSELF!

Please redeem ALL sin, disobedience, and wickedness in our lives (past, present, and future, permanently and FOREVER!) – for Your holy, holy, HOLY Name's sake, Jesus! – with endtime ANOINTINGS in unlimited measure, such as this world has never seen before! We soak this prayer in the blood of Jesus, the holy anointing

oil of the Holy Ghost, and the fire of God, in Jesus' Name!
Amen!

II Peter 3:18

18. But grow in the grace and knowledge of our Lord and
Savior Jesus Christ. To Him be glory both now and
forever! Amen.

Dear Holy, Mighty, and Amazing God, there is NONE like
You! It is YOU ONLY that we adore! HOLY and JUST are
ALL Your ways! The WHOLE earth is FILLED with Your
glory! ALL PRAISE belongs to the KING of all kings and
the LORD of all lords! HALLELUIAH!

We SO want to be like YOU, JESUS! So we HUMBLY ask
You now to help us GROW in the grace and knowledge
of our Lord and Savior, Jesus Christ! POUR OUT Your
Holy Ghost "Miracle-Grow" upon us in UNLIMITED
MEASURE, and SATURATE US (COMPLETELY and
FOREVER!) with Your holy PRESENCE! – so that we
SPROUT UP (to UNBELIEVABLE HEIGHTS!) literally
OVERNIGHT! HALLELUIAH!

We give YOU ALL the glory, both now and FOREVER!
AMEN!

We HUMBLY ask You now, dear Jesus, to REDEEM all things that have ever, ever, EVER kept us from growing in You (past, present, and future, permanently and FOREVER!) – for Your honor and Your glory ALONE! – with ENDTIME ANOINTINGS in UNLIMITED MEASURE, such as this world has NEVER SEEN BEFORE! We SOAK this prayer in the BLOOD of Jesus, the HOLY anointing oil of the Holy Ghost, and the FIRE of God, in JESUS' NAME! AMEN!

Bonus - #1

Dear Holy and Sovereign Lord of ALL, we HUMBLY come before Your Presence with a very, very, VERY special request today. We are worn out from these constant battles! Help us, we pray! Move heaven and earth to save us and redeem us – for Your holy, holy, holy Name's sake! Do what only You can do! Fight for us with Your MIGHTY, MIGHTY, MIGHTY hand, oh Lord! Have MERCY upon us, we pray! PULL our feet from the miry clay! SET us on the Solid Rock (Jesus Christ!)! You are our Defender, Protector, and Judge! Redeem all of this mess (from the enemy) for Your Name's sake, we pray! Turn it all around for YOUR GLORY and our good, as You promised You would (in Your holy Word!)!

Please redeem all battles against us (past, present, and future, permanently and forever!) – for Your holy, precious Name's sake! – with endtime anointings in unlimited measure, such as this world has never seen before! We soak this prayer in the BLOOD of Jesus, the HOLY anointing oil of the Holy Ghost, and the FIRE of God, in Jesus' Name! AMEN!

Bonus - #2

Dear God Almighty, Lord of heaven and earth and of all that exists, we HUMBLY come before You with hearts ablaze for YOU! We desire YOU above all else! Fill us to OVERFLOWING with Your PRESENCE, we pray! – in the mighty, precious, and holy Name of JESUS, King of kings and Lord of lords! HALLELUIAH!

We HUMBLY ask You now, dear Lord, to MULTIPLY our prayers times twelve! – in the mighty, precious, and holy Name of JESUS, Lord of lords and King of kings! This is absolutely NO PROBLEM (at all!) for You to do, oh Mighty One of Israel! YOU parted the Red Sea for the Israelites, so YOU can certainly multiply the power of our humble prayers we offer to You today! Infuse them with YOUR super-charged, Holy Ghost POWER so that they EXPLODE into the atmosphere, drastically, dramatically, and INSTANTLY changing lives and circumstances! (past, present, and future, permanently and FOREVER!) - for Your holy and precious Name's sake, Sweet JESUS! HALLELUIAH! Let ALL the earth rejoice in Christ, her SAVIOR! AMEN!

We HUMBLY ask You now, dear JESUS, to REDEEM all of our weak and ineffective prayers! (past, present, and future, permanently and forever!) – with endtime ANOINTINGS in UNLIMITED measure, such as this world has NEVER SEEN BEFORE! We soak this prayer in the BLOOD of Jesus, the HOLY anointing oil of the Holy Ghost, and the FIRE of God, in JESUS' NAME! AMEN!

Bonus - #3

Dear God of the angel armies, You are always by my side! You are always more than a friend to me! You have my back like no other person ever could, ever has, or ever will! HALLELUIAH! All glory to the Lord of Hosts! Great and mighty are all Your holy ways, oh KING of the UNIVERSE! We bow down to You and worship You ALONE, proclaiming You as Lord of all! Holy, holy, holy are You, oh Lord God ALMIGHTY!

Dear God, we HUMBLY come before You to request a special favor today! You see how many evil prayers have been prayed against us, so we are asking You now to redeem every single one (past, present, and future, permanently and FOREVER!) – for Your holy, precious Name's sake! – with endtime ANOINTINGS in unlimited measure, such as this world has never seen BEFORE! We SOAK this prayer in the blood of Jesus, the holy anointing oil of the Holy Ghost, and the fire of God, in Jesus' Name! AMEN!

Bonus - #4

Dear Lord God of all, we HUMBLY come before You this day with heavy hearts. You see how many attacks we have had against our health (ADD, autism, scoliosis, insomnia, inflammation, kidney/liver issues, sight/hearing issues, heart and thyroid issues, premature aging, obesity, and injuries). However, we know that You are the God who HEALS, DELIVERS, and REDEEMS, and we know that You are the ONLY ONE WHO CAN! HALLELUIAH! So we are calling upon the VERY HIGHEST SOURCE POSSIBLE to aid us in our deep distress! You know full-well that we have completely exhausted all of our resources in attempting to cure any and all of these conditions, and we have been 100% unsuccessful! So YOU are our very last and ONLY HOPE, JESUS! Without You, we can do absolutely nothing at all! We are well aware of our human frailty! So, Sweet Jesus, please lend Your ear to our constant cries for help and have compassion upon us, we pray! Please cancel, undo, and destroy all of the works of the enemy (with regards to our health); and completely REDEEM these attacks (against our health)! – past, present, and future, PERMANENTLY and FOREVER! – with ENDTIME ANOINTINGS in UNLIMITED MEASURE, such as this world has NEVER SEEN BEFORE! We SOAK this prayer in

the BLOOD of Jesus, the HOLY anointing oil of the Holy
Ghost, and the FIRE of God, in JESUS' NAME! AMEN!

Bonus - #5

Dear Lord God of Everything – that is, that was and that is to come – we PRAISE Your holy, precious, mighty Name, for YOU are worthy of our everything! NOTHING exists apart from YOU! You "own the cattle on a thousand hills"! You created all things and sustain all things! Glory to Your precious, awesome, mighty Name, oh Jehovah, KING of all!

Our humble request today is simple: to COMPLETELY, ABSOLUTELY, and OVERWHELMINGLY FLOOD us with Your UNLIMITED wealth! – in the precious, holy, and mighty Name of Jesus, King of kings and Lord of lords! – for YOUR holy Kingdom's purposes "on earth, as it is in heaven"!

You see how much the enemy has stolen from us time and time and time again, and we know that You are a God of justice! So we HUMBLY implore You to "make all things right", by returning to us (a thousand-fold) anything and everything that the enemy even thought about stealing from us, in the mighty, precious, and holy Name of KING JESUS!

Please redeem ALL WEALTH that has EVER, EVER, EVER been stolen from us! (past, present, and future, PERMANENTLY and FOREVER!), in the mighty, precious, and HOLY NAME of JESUS – the King who reigns FOREVERMORE! HALLELUIAH! – with endtime ANOINTINGS in UNLIMITED MEASURE, such as this world has NEVER SEEN BEFORE! We SOAK this prayer in the BLOOD of Jesus, the HOLY anointing oil of the Holy Ghost, and the FIRE of God, in Jesus' Name. AMEN.

Torrents & Torrents & Torrents

Bonus - #6

Dear Lord God of heaven and earth, who is like our God?!? YOU stand alone as the One and Only True GOD! HALLELUIAH! All other "gods" are false and dead! ONLY YOU are the "Real Deal"! All glory to Your holy, precious, and matchless Name, oh JEHOVAH!

We HUMBLY come before You with a request that is very "near and dear" to my heart, Jesus! You know that we are living in the end times, where it will be CRITICAL that we KNOW the Word of God! – for it is "living and active, sharper than any double-edged sword, penetrating even to dividing the soul and spirit, the joints and marrow"! HALLELUIAH! Your living, holy Word, oh God, truly is an essential weapon that we need to overcome and obliterate the powers of darkness!

You know, oh God, that I have been diligently crying out (to You) for the miraculous gift of Your Word (from Genesis through Revelation) to be permanently and FOREVER implanted deep within me! I need to have it FULLY and COMPLETELY memorized, as well as be able to FULLY and COMPLETELY understand it! HALLELUIAH!

You say that "all things are possible with You", so I am believing (with simple child-like faith) that this one request truly is 100% possible with You, Jesus! AMEN!

We HUMBLY ask You now, dear Jesus, to redeem anything and everything that has ever, ever, EVER kept us from FULLY and COMPLETELY knowing and understanding Your most holy Word (the Bible)! – with endtime ANOINTINGS in UNLIMITED MEASURE, such as this world has NEVER SEEN BEFORE! We SOAK this prayer in the BLOOD of JESUS, the HOLY anointing oil of the HOLY GHOST, and the FIRE of GOD, in Jesus' Name! AMEN!

Bonus - #7

Dear Most Holy and Sovereign Creator of all, we HUMBLY come to You today with a VERY NECESSARY request. So very MANY of us have been DEEPLY wounded (emotionally) in this past season, especially by close friends and family. HOWEVER, we know that OUR GOD is FAR GREATER than anything the enemy could ever throw at us! HALLELUIAH! So we are asking You now, oh GREAT CREATOR of heaven and earth, to THOROUGHLY, COMPLETELY, and FULLY heal ALL of our soul wounds, down to the VERY DEEPEST level POSSIBLE! (past, present, and future, PERMANENTLY and FOREVER!) – in the precious, mighty, and matchless Name of Jesus, Lord Most HIGH! AMEN!

We do not want to give the enemy ANY OPENING (in our lives) WHATSOEVER! So we FREELY CHOOSE to RELEASE ALL hurt, anger, bitterness, or regret into Your arms and LEAVE IT THERE! HALLELUIAH! We KNOW that Your GREATEST DESIRE (for Your children) is to see them set free from the chains that have bound them for so long! In exchange for our pain, You freely offer us Your peace that passes ALL understanding, Your

147

UNCONTAINABLE joy, Your hope that ENDURES to the end, and Your UNCONDITIONAL love! AMEN!

So we CHOOSE YOU, JESUS, and EVERYTHING that YOU have to offer us! We FREELY forgive those who have sinned against us and show them the same grace that You so FREELY showed to us! – when You died on the cross for us and set us ETERNALLY FREE, in Jesus' Name! AMEN!

We HUMBLY ask You now, Precious Savior, to redeem ALL of our soul wounds (past, present, and future, PERMANENTLY and FOREVER!)! – for Your holy, precious Name's sake, dear Jesus! – with endtime ANOINTINGS in UNLIMITED MEASURE, such as this world has NEVER SEEN BEFORE! We SOAK this prayer in the BLOOD of Jesus, the HOLY anointing oil of the Holy Ghost, and the FIRE of God, in Jesus' Name! AMEN!

A.

Dear Holy and Mighty God of ALL THINGS, WORTHY is Your Name in ALL the earth! YOU are seated above ALL THINGS! Earth is Your footstool! When You speak, the earth SHAKES! GLORY to the KING ETERNAL! – who is, who was, and who is to come! HALLELUIAH!

We bow down before YOU and worship the KING! You ALONE are our Commander-in-Chief! YOU give the orders, and we will GLADLY and WILLINGLY follow YOU all the days of our lives and FOREVER! AMEN!

Oh, GREAT and MIGHTY JEHOVAH, we HUMBLY come before YOU today to request Your FULL, DIVINE PROTECTION! We KNOW that YOU hold the world in Your hand, and ABSOLUTELY NOTHING is too big or too hard for YOU to do, oh CAPTAIN of the angel armies! HALLELUIAH! So we are calling upon the VERY HIGHEST POWER that exists to come to our aid! We HUMBLY ask You to defend us and protect us as NOBODY ELSE CAN! PLEASE be our Shield, for YOU ALONE are our EVERYTHING! Put an IMPENETRABLE "Holy Ghost bubble" around us COMPLETELY (PERMANENTLY and

FOREVER!) so that we are 100% INVISIBLE to the enemy! And while the enemy will NOT be able to see us AT ALL, PLEASE make him 100% EXPOSED so that he can be taken out QUICKLY and COMPLETELY! – to bring ALL honor, glory, and adoration to Your holy, precious, and mighty Name, KING JESUS! HALLELUIAH!

We HUMBLY ask You now, dear Jesus, to redeem ALL of the times that we have ever been unprotected and exposed to the enemy (past, present, and future, PERMANENTLY and FOREVER!) – to the honor and glory of Your holy and precious Name! – with endtime anointings in UNLIMITED MEASURE, such as this world has NEVER SEEN BEFORE! We SOAK this prayer in the BLOOD of Jesus, the HOLY anointing oil of the Holy Ghost, and the FIRE of God, in JESUS' NAME! AMEN!

B.

Dear Lord God ALMIGHTY, MAKER of heaven and earth and of all that exists, WORTHY is Your Name in ALL the earth! The WHOLE EARTH is FULL of Your glory! PRAISES to the King of all kings! HALLELUIAH!

We HUMBLY call upon YOU to rescue us, DEAR GOD, from ALL of the traps of the enemy! YOU see how he lies in wait to try to snare us time and time and time again!   DELIVER us from his clutches, OH GOD! PUNISH him SEVERELY for his innumerable harassments, we pray! Make him COMPLETELY REGRET the day he started causing trouble for the children of the MOST HIGH GOD! AMEN!

YOU ALONE are our DEFENDER! There is ABSOLUTELY NOONE ELSE that we can call upon in our time of great distress! ONLY YOU can move heaven and earth to snatch us from the enemy's grasp! HALLELUIAH! So we are FULLY COUNTING ON YOU to "make a way where there is no way"! PULL us out of the miry clay, and SET our feet upon the Solid Rock (JESUS CHRIST!)!

Please redeem ANYTHING and EVERYHTING that has EVER snared or trapped us (past, present, and future, PERMANENTLY and FOREVER!) – for Your holy and precious Name's sake, SWEET JESUS! – with endtime ANOINTINGS in UNLIMITED MEASURE, such as this world has NEVER SEEN BEFORE! We SOAK this prayer in the blood of Jesus, the holy anointing oil of the Holy Ghost, and the fire of God, in JESUS' NAME. AMEN.

C.

Dear God Most High, WORTHY is Your Name in ALL the earth! HOLY and JUST are ALL Your ways, oh JEHOVAH! We bow down before You to WORSHIP and ADORE the King who REIGNS on HIGH, both NOW and FOREVERMORE! AMEN!

We HUMBLY ask You now, DEAR JESUS, to COMPLETELY EXPOSE EACH and EVERY PLAN of the enemy! Please LAY BARE ALL of his EVIL INTENTS, and COMPLETELY TURN them BACK ON TO HIS OWN HEAD, in the precious, holy, and mighty Name of JESUS, KING of kings and LORD of lords! HALLELUIAH!

Only YOU can THOROUGHLY CLENASE our land of the devil's works! (GREAT and MIGHTY are ALL Your holy ways, OH JEHOVAH!) We HUMBLY ask You now, DEAR JESUS, to put an IMMEDIATE and COMPLETE STOP to ALL the works of iniquity! (past, present, and future, PERMANENTLY and FOREVER!)! AMEN!

We THANK YOU, SWEET JESUS, for "stepping in" and putting a PERMANENT STOP to ALL of this NONSENSE that we have had to ENDURE FOR SO LONG! THANK YOU for RESCUING us from the den of wolves, where the enemy ONLY sought to tear us apart and destroy us! We are SO GRATEFUL that YOU, OH LORD, had MUCH DIFFERENT (AND GREATER!) plans for us! HALLELUIAH! ALL GLORY belongs to the KING ETERNAL, forever and ever and ever! AMEN!

Please redeem ALL evil things that have been hidden (past, present, and future, permanently and forever!) – for Your Name's sake, SWEET JESUS! – with endtime ANOINTINGS in unlimited measure, such as this world has NEVER SEEN BEFORE! We SOAK this prayer in the BLOOD of Jesus, the HOLY anointing oil of the Holy Ghost, and the FIRE of God, in JESUS' NAME! AMEN!

Graduation Day!

Dearest Holy God MOST HIGH, we HUMBLY come before Your Presence with thanksgiving and into Your courts with praise! We PRAISE Your holy, precious Name and DECLARE that You are LORD and KING!!! There is NONE as beautiful and glorious and magnificent as YOU, OH LORD GOD MOST HIGH! Even "the heavens declare Your glory, and the firmament shows Your handiwork"! Strength and honor belong to YOU ALONE! AMEN!

We are VERY EXCITED about today, dear Lord! We have waited our ENTIRE LIVES for this moment! We have dreamed, waited, and prayed for this day to arrive! And now that it is here, we can HARDLY BELIEVE IT! It is as if we are in a dream! GLORY to Your holy, precious Name, oh MIGHTY ONE OF ISRAEL!

THANK YOU, oh God, for FAITHFULLY carrying us this far! You were with us EACH and EVERY step of the way! When we grew weary, YOU strengthened us and reminded us that we "CAN do ALL THINGS through CHRIST WHO GIVES US STRENGTH"! HALLELUIAH!!!

THANK YOU for PATIENTLY working with us and teaching us Your precious, holy ways! You invested COUNTLESS hours and amounts of energy and love into us! You NEVER gave up on us, even when we wanted to give up on ourselves! HALLELUIAH!!!

So we HUMBLY ask You now, dear Savior, to PRMOTE US (RIGHT NOW, INSTANTLY!!!) to the VERY HIGHEST LEVEL POSSIBLE – in the precious, holy, and mighty Name of Jesus, KING of kings and LORD of lords!!! HALLELUIAH!!!

PLEASE REDEEM EACH and EVERY STOLEN PROMOTION IN OUR LIVES (PAST, PRESENT, and FUTURE, PERMANENLTY and FOREVER!) – in the HOLY, PRECIOUS, and MIGHTY NAME OF JESUS! – with ENDTIME ANOINTINGS in UNLIMITED MEASURE, SUCH AS THIS WORLD HAS NEVER SEEN BEFORE! We SOAK this prayer in the BLOOD of JESUS, the HOLY anointing oil of the HOLY GHOST, and the FIRE of GOD, in JESUS' NAME! AMEN!

Rejoice! – Victory Forevermore!!!

Dearest Holy and Sovereign God MOST HIGH, WORTHY is Your Name in ALL THE EARTH! All honor, glory and power belong to YOU ALONE! It is YOU ALONE we adore, worship, and desire ABOVE ALL ELSE! You ONLY are our strength, our song, and our salvation! HALLELUIAH!!!

We thank You that "You hold VICTORY in store for the upright", and "NO GOOD THING will YOU withhold from those who put their trust in You"! YOU are the faithful God who takes care of His own! HALLELUIAH!!!

So we HUMBLY ask You now, DEAR JESUS, to POUR OUT UPON US (in UNLIMITED MEASURE!) Your VICTORY in ALL aspects of our lives – spiritually, mentally, physically, relationally, business-wise, ministry-wise, and financially! – in the precious, mighty Name of JESUS, King of kings and Lord of lords! HALLELUIAH!!!

We HUMBLY ask You now, DEAR JESUS, to redeem ALL LOSSES in our lives (PAST, PRESENT, and FUTURE,

PERMANENTLY and FOREVER!) – in the HOLY, PRECIOUS, and MIGHTY NAME OF JESUS! – with ENDTIME ANOINTINGS in UNLIMITED MEASURE, SUCH AS THIS WORLD HAS NEVER SEEN BEFORE! We SOAK this prayer in the BLOOD of JESUS, the HOLY anointing oil of the HOLY GHOST, and the FIRE of GOD, in JESUS' NAME! AMEN!

Lydia

REDEEM

Our Promised Land

Dearest Holy and Sovereign God of ALL, we worship, adore, and magnify Your holy, precious NAME! Let ALL the earth rejoice in Christ her Savior! AMEN! There is NONE like our precious Jesus! HOLY and JUST are ALL Your ways, oh MIGHTY ONE of ISRAEL!

We thank You for safely bringing us this far! The journey has been long and hard, but YOU, OH LORD, FAITHFULLY sustained us! What an AMAZING, AWESOME GOD we serve! HALLELUIAH!

We JOYFULLY exalt and lift Your Name on high! Let the floodgates of our praises OPEN WIDE, so that YOU may be FULLY honored and glorified FOREVER and EVER and EVER! AMEN!

We HUMBLY ask You now, oh Lord, to SAFELY carry us the rest of the way! We KNOW that there are MANY BATTLES AHEAD of us, which can ONLY be WON if YOU FIGHT FOR US! HALLELUIAH! So we are calling upon the VERY HIGHEST POWER that exists to go before us and ANNIHILATE the enemy (COMPLETELY and FOREVER!) – in the precious, mighty, and holy Name of JESUS!

Please redeem ALL BATTLES that we have lost (PAST, PRESENT, and FUTURE, PERMANENTLY and FOREVER!) – in the PRECIOUS, HOLY, and MIGHTY NAME OF JESUS, LORD OF HOSTS! – with ENDTIME ANOINTINGS in UNLIMITED MEASURE, such as this world has NEVER SEEN BEFORE! We SOAK this prayer in the BLOOD of JESUS, the HOLY anointing oil of the HOLY GHOST, and the FIRE of GOD, in JESUS' NAME! AMEN!

The Spinning Top

Dearest Holy God MOST HIGH, we HUMBLY come
before You with grateful hearts! Only YOU can free us
from all the junk thrown at us our entire lives! We
KNOW that You have already begun "spinning the top"
in order to fling off of us all the garbage! – so that it can
never stick to us again, in the precious Name of Jesus,
King of kings and Lord of lords! HALLELUIAH!

We KNOW that "if the Son makes us free, then we are
free indeed"! So we are anxious to FULLY experience the
TRUE FREEDOM that can ONLY come through YOU,
SWEET JESUS! Wash us SO COMPLETELY until we are as
white as snow, we pray – in the precious, matchless
Name of King Jesus!

WORTHY are You, oh Lord God Most High, to receive
ALL honor and glory and praise! We WORSHIP You
ALONE and EXALT Your holy Name! ALL creation
SHOUTS Your praises! HALLELUIAH!

THANK YOU for what You are doing in our lives! We EAGERLY look forward to ALL the debris of the past being gone FOREVER! AMEN! We KNOW that as You speed up the "top", hurts, disappointments, curses, addictions, sins, ungodly ties, and unhealthy thought processes will FLY off FASTER and THICKER! HALLELUIAH!

We ask You now, dear Jesus, to please redeem ALL of these evil things that have ever, ever, ever attached themselves to us – in the precious, mighty, and matchless Name of Jesus, Lord God Most High – with endtime anointings in UNLIMITED MEASURE, such as this world has NEVER SEEN BEFORE! We SOAK this prayer in the BLOOD of Jesus, the HOLY anointing oil of the Holy Ghost, and the FIRE of God, in Jesus' Name. Amen.

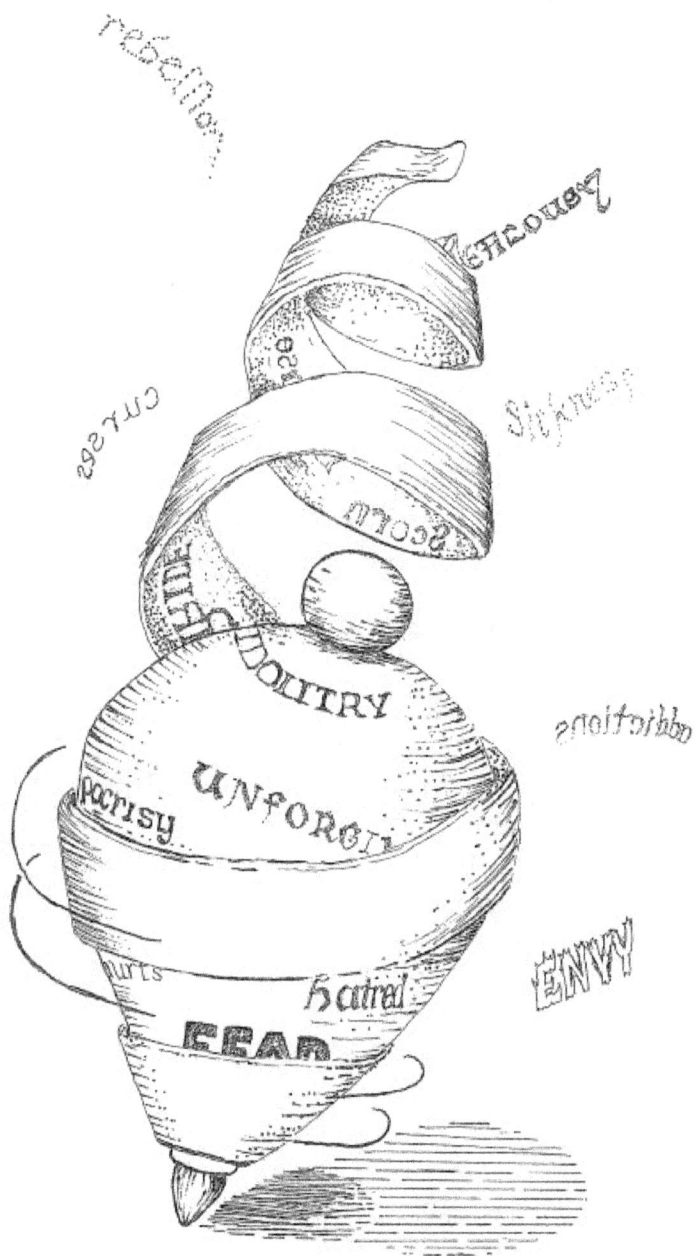

About the Author

Heather Howard is simply a child of the King. Through the many trials in life, she has ALWAYS seen God remain faithful and true to HIS promises, which cannot EVER fail! When "the going got tough," she started praying and watched God turn things around for His glory and her good ... and not always as she expected! His ways may surprise us, but they are always the best ways!

Her passion is to be fully used by God for His purposes alone! There is no greater fulfillment or satisfaction than that! Halleluiah! She loves to see the Body of Christ coming into its full maturity and strives to do what she can to enable that. She is praying wholeheartedly for every reader of this book to grow into the fullness of what God has planned for them! All glory belongs to our precious Lord and Savior, Jesus Christ!

She encourages you to be a "Peter" today - jump out of the safety of the boat, and "walk on water" with Jesus, by faith! Don't look at the "waves" of life, but rather, keep your eyes focused on JESUS ALONE! He ONLY is your Source, and He WILL provide! He is your Rock, and HE will uphold you with His righteous right hand forevermore! Halleluiah! and Amen!!! ☺

You can reach us at:

www.FruitfulMinistries.org   OR

fruitfulministries@outlook.com